Best Practices of

Award-Winning ELEMENTARY SCHOOL Principals

SANDRA
HARRIS

Best
Practices
of
Award-
Winning
ELEMENTARY SCHOOL
Principals

FOREWORD BY
VINCENT FERRANDINO

CORWIN PRESS
A SAGE Publications Company
Thousand Oaks, California

For information:

Corwin Press
A Sage Publications Company
2455 Teller Road
Thousand Oaks, California 91320
www.corwinpress.com

Sage Publications Ltd.
1 Oliver's Yard
55 City Road
London EC1Y 1SP
United Kingdom

Sage Publications India Pvt. Ltd.
B-42, Panchsheel Enclave
Post Box 4109
New Delhi 110 017 India

Printed in the United States of America

Library of Congress Cataloging-in-Publication Data

Harris, Sandra, 1946-
Best practices of award-winning elementary school principals / Sandra Harris.
    p. cm.
Includes bibliographical references and index.
ISBN 1–4129–0647–4 (cloth) — ISBN 1–4129–0648–2 (pbk.)
    1. Elementary school principals—United States—Case studies.
2. School improvement programs—United States—Case studies. 3. Educational leadership—United States—Case studies. I. Title.
LB2831.82.H37 2005
372.12'012—dc22   2004029803

This book is printed on acid-free paper.

05   06   07   08   09   10   9   8   7   6   5   4   3   2   1

Acquisitions Editor:	Elizabeth Brenkus
Editorial Assistant:	Candice L. Ling
Production Editor:	Laureen A. Shea
Copy Editor:	Barbara Coster
Typesetter:	C&M Digitals (P) Ltd.
Proofreader:	Christine Dahlin
Indexer:	Pamela Van Huss
Cover Designer:	Rose Storey
Graphic Designer:	Lisa Miller

Contents

Foreword

What a pleasure to be part of this important book that speaks directly to principals in precisely the method they appreciate the most—advice and counsel from their peers. It's a great honor to be able to introduce the wise words of outstanding and award-winning school leaders, most of whom I know well and respect enormously.

I was taken, but not surprised, by the totally child-centered approach each contributor to this book took as he or she discussed successes on the job. Principals stress treating all children with dignity. They always place children before all else. Next come their staffs and their families and, finally, themselves. In my experience, great principals tend to be humble but steely strong leaders who give credit to others. But they are always in the background making the tough decisions, doing what's best for children, and backing up their staffs.

For over two decades, we have heard this when our National Distinguished Principals come to Washington, D.C., for this most prestigious award presented by the National Association of Elementary School Principals and the U.S. Department of Education. As they accept the award, they always point out how much help they've had along the way. But we know that it's *their* decisions, drive, and dedication that set the tone and create the climate of their outstanding schools. Furthermore, the glitter of the award is quickly pushed aside as they eagerly share their best practices and eagerly learn all they can from their esteemed colleagues from across the country and around the world.

This book overflows with ways to keep standards and staff morale high. The principals define customer-friendly schools and illustrate how sharing decisions with staff makes schools stronger. They explain how to help children *belong* in their schools rather than just attend. However, their advice doesn't end with the final bell. They truly welcome and understand how to help struggling students, at-risk youngsters, non-English speakers, and the many children who need far more time and attention than schools are expected to offer.

In 2001, the National Association of Elementary School Principals published a landmark report, *Leading Learning Communities: What Principals Should Know and Be Able to Do*, as a guide to principals in crafting their responsibilities in key instructional areas. Without a doubt, the contributors to this book know what to do, how to do it, and when to do it!

Vincent Ferrandino
Executive Director
National Association of Elementary School Principals

Acknowledgments

I remember well the day that Robb Clouse askèd if I would be interested in authoring a book of best practice ideas from award-winning elementary school principals. Not only did it seem like a great idea, it seemed to be something that would come together very easily. All I had to do was e-mail award-winning principals and ask them to submit their great ideas. I expected my in-box to be full immediately. But principals are busy, and award-winning principals are even busier! A project that I expected to take just a few months has taken over 12 months to complete. But it has resulted in over 100 best practice ideas from 35 award-winning elementary school principals who took time away from their busy schedules to share thoughtful, insightful ideas with their colleagues and aspiring elementary school principals.

Just when I thought the manuscript was finished and couldn't get any better, the reviewers gave their suggestions. Many of their excellent ideas were incorporated into the book.

I want to acknowledge the creative advice and direction from my editor, Lizzie Brenkus, and the help from Candice Ling. Their communication skills, encouragement, and support deserve awards.

Thank you, award-winning principals, reviewers, Candice, Lizzie, and Robb. This project took longer than I anticipated, but the final product is better than I had imagined. It's a winner!

Sandy Harris

About the Author

 **Sandra Harris** is currently associate professor and director of the doctoral program in Educational Leadership at Lamar University in Beaumont, Texas, where she teaches classes in social justice, action research, and other administrator preparation courses. Formerly, she served as a teacher, principal, and superintendent in public and private schools. Her scholarship agenda includes administrator preparation, K–12 peer harassment, and building relationship-oriented, socially-just school environments. She publishes and presents at regional, state, and national conferences on these topics.

About the Contributors

Kim Boelkes
kboelkes@cantonusd.org
Eastview Elementary School
1490 East Myrtle
Canton, IL 61520
Principal: 13 years
School Population: 500 students
Grades: K–4
2003 NCLB Blue Ribbon School
2003 IPA Western Region Principal of the Year
2003 Canton Woman of the Year

Stephany Bourne
Stephany.Bourne@ fwcs.k12.in.us
Indian Village Elementary School
3835 Wenonah Lane
Ft. Wayne, IN 46809
Head of School: 6 years
School Population: 385 students
Grades: PK–5
2003 NCLB Blue Ribbon School
2001 Model School of Improvement—Illinois State Dept. of Education

John Ciesluk
jciesluk@longmeadow.k12.ma.us
Wolf Swamp Road Elementary School
62 Wolf Swamp Road
Longmeadow, MA 01355
Principal: 25 years
School Population: 475 students
Grades: K–4
2003 National Distinguished Principal
2001–2002 Massachusetts Compass School nominee

Dan Coram
dcoram@access.k12.wv.us
Steenrod Elementary School
100 Clarks Lane
Wheeling, WV 26003
Principal: 18 years
School Population: 270 students
Grades: K–5
2003 NCLB Blue Ribbon School

Cynthia Eliser
Celiser.rles@lafourche.k12.la.us
Raceland Lower Elementary School
4101 Highway 308, Post Office Box 529
Raceland, LA 70394
Principal: 9 years
School Population: 389 students
Grades: PreK–2
2002 National Distinguished Principal

Robert W. Fowls
Bob.fowls@saints.org
Trinity Lutheran School
2250 North East Butler Market Road
Bend, OR 97701
Principal: 11 years
School Population: 325 students
Grades: PreK–8
2003 National Distinguished Principal

Cindy Gipson
cgipson@hinds.k12.ms.us
Raymond Elementary School
417 Palestine Road
Raymond, MS 39154
Principal: 8 years
School Population: 486 students
Grades: K–6
2003 National Distinguished Principal

Orquidia Hathaway
hathawayo@svusd.k12.ca.us
Ralph A. Gates Charter Language Academy
23882 Landisview Avenue
Lake Forest, CA 92630
2003 California School Boards Golden Bell Program
Principal: 6 years
School Population: 812 students
Grades: K–6
2004 NCLB Blue Ribbon School
2003 State Title I Achieving School
2003 USDOE Successful Charter School
2002 California Distinguished School

Kathleen Genovese Haworth
kathleenhaworth@laurelhall.com
Laurel Hall School
11919 Oxnard Street
North Hollywood, CA 91606
Head of School: 7 years
School Population: 570 students
Grades: K–8
2003 Steve Allen Educational Excellence Award
2003 Nova Southeastern/NAESP National Fellow Scholarship
2002 National Distinguished Principal

Scott Hollinger
Scott.hollinger@mcallenisd.net
McAuliffe Elementary School
3000 Daffodil Avenue
McAllen, TX 78501
Principal: 11 years
School Population: 800 students
Grades: PS–5
2003 National Distinguished Principal

Rick Ivers
ivers@amigo.net
Manassa Elementary School
2611 Park Avenue
Alamosa, CO 81101
Principal: 7 years
School Population: 232 students
Grades: K–5
2003 NCLB Blue Ribbon School

Gloria L. Kumagai
gloria.kumagai@spps.org
Museum Magnet Elementary School
560 Concordia Avenue
St. Paul, MN 55103
Principal: 17 years
School Population: 330 students
Grades: K–6
2002 National Distinguished Principal
2001 NCLB Blue Ribbon School

Carol J. Lark
cjlark@interact.ccsd.net
C. P. Squires Elementary School
1312 East Tonopah
North Las Vegas, NV 89030
Principal: 14 years
School Population: 947 students
Grades: PreK–5
2003 National Distinguished Principal
2001 Model School Award
2001 Congressional Award–Outstanding Improvements in a School Year
Ms. Lark is currently assistant superintendent for North Las Vegas ISD.

Carol Loflin
Cloflin922@comcast.net
Twin Creeks Elementary School
2785 Marsh Drive
San Ramon, CA 94583-2049
Principal: 7 years
School Population: 450 students
Grades: K–5
2003 NCLB Blue Ribbon School
2002 California Distinguished School

Karen Lyon
klyon@stbarnabasofdeland.org
St. Barnabas Episcopal School
322 West Michigan Avenue
DeLand, FL 32720
Head of School: 9 years
School Population: 364 students
Grades: PreK–8
2003 NCLB Blue Ribbon School

Exerta T. Mackie
emackie@houstonisd.org
Kashmere Gardens Elementary School
4901 Lockwood
Houston, TX 77026
Principal: 5 years
School Population: 510 students
Grades: PreK–6
2003 NCLB Blue Ribbon School

Marla W. McGhee
mmcghee@austin.rr.com
Live Oak Elementary School
8607 Anderson Mill Road
Austin, TX 78729
Principal: 7 years
School Population: 500 students
Grades: EC–5
1995 Principal in Residence, U.S. Department of Education Finalist
1994 National Distinguished Principal
1992 NCLB Blue Ribbon School
Dr. McGhee is currently codirector of the National Center for School
    Improvement at Texas State University, San Marcos, TX.

Lori Musser
lmusser@joplin.k12.mo.us
Columbia Elementary School
610 West F Street
Joplin, MO 64801
Principal: 3 years
School Population: 275 students
Grades: K–5
2003–2004 Missouri Gold Star School Award
2003 NCLB Blue Ribbon School

Elizabeth Neale
Deneale6@hotmail.com
Silvio O. Conte Community School
200 West Union Street
Pittsfield, MA 01201
Principal: 17 years
School Population: 500 students
Grades: PreK–5
2002 National Distinguished Principal

Keith Owen
kowen@du.edu
Beulah Heights Elementary School
2670 Delphinium Street
Pueblo, CO 81005
Principal: 6 years
School Population: 350 students
Grades: PreK–5
2003 National Distinguished Principal

Michele Pecina
Pecina_m@madera.k12.ca.us
James Monroe Year-Round Elementary School
1819 North Lake Street
Madera, CA 93638
Principal: 14 years
School Population: 970 students
Grades: K–6
2003 National Distinguished Principal
2003 Soroptomist Woman of the Year
Two California School Board Association Golden Bell Awards
1997 California Distinguished School Award

Ann Porter, Retired
mgporter@gra.mdco.net
3623 Kimberly Court
Grand Forks, ND 58201
Principal: 13 years
School Population: 225 students
Grades: K–5
2002 National Distinguished Principal

Jane Hoskins Roberts
jroberts@kcs.kana.k12.wv.us
Alban Elementary School
2030 Harrison Avenue
St. Albans, WV 25177
Principal: 9 years
School Population: 344 students
Grades: K–5
2001 Kanawha County Schools Principal of the Year
2001 State Farm Premiere Principal Award
1999–2001West Virginia Title I Distinguished School

Sharon Roemer
SRoemer@lmusd.org
Ocean View Elementary School
1208 Linda Drive
Arroyo Grande, CA 93420
Principal: 7 years
School Population: 575 students
Grades: K–6
2003 NCLB National Blue Ribbon School
2002 California Distinguished School

Gina Segobiano
ginasego@stclair.k12.il.us
Signal Hill Elementary School
40 Signal Hill Place
Belleville, IL 62223
Principal: 10 years
School Population: 430 students
Grades: K–8
2002 National Distinguished Principal
Ms. Segobiano is currently superintendent/principal at Signal Hill School
    District #181.

Dawn Smith
dsmith@509j.net
Warm Springs Elementary School
Warm Springs Indian Reservation
Post Office Box 886
Warm Springs, OR 97761
Principal: 10 years
School Population: 400 students
Grades: K–5
2003 National Distinguished Principal
1999 Semifinalist, U.S. Department of Education Professional
    Development

Rod Smith
mcsmith@smsd.org
Mill Creek Elementary School
13951 West 79th Street
Lenexa, KS 66215
Principal: 4 years
School Population: 445 students
Grades: K–6
2003 NCLB Blue Ribbon School

Gene M. Solomon
gsolom@optonline.net
E. A. Cavallini Middle School
392 West Saddle River Road
Upper Saddle River, NJ 07458
Principal: 8 years
School Population: 450 students
Grades: 6–8
2003 National Distinguished Principal

Mary Kay Sommers
msommers@psdschools.org
Shepardson Elementary School
1501 Springwood Drive
Fort Collins, CO 80528
Principal: 15 years
School Population: 500 students
Grades: K–6
2003–2006 NAESP Board of Directors, Zone 7
2000–2003 John Irwin School of Excellence Award–Colorado
Semifinalist, National 21st Century School of Excellence

Ursina Swanson
Ursinaswanson@comcast.net
Park Spanish Immersion School
6300 Walker Street
St. Louis Park, MN 55416–2382
Principal: 6 years
School Population: 540 students
Grades: K–6
2003 NCLB Blue Ribbon School
Commendation—Office of Governor
2001 Outstanding Administrator, Organization of American Kodály
   Music Educators

Ramona S. Trevino
ramonatrev@yahoo.com
Zilker Elementary School
1900 Bluebonnet Lane
Austin, TX 78702
Principal: 9 years
School Population: 504 students
Grades: PS–6
2001 Model Site for Principles of Learning
2000 National Pilot School, Technology Resource Learning
1999 & 2000 Texas Successful Schools Award
1999 Best Elementary School in Austin
1998 U.S. National Blue Ribbon School
Ms. Trevino is currently principal at the University of Texas Elementary
School in Austin, TX.

Sharon L. Vestermark
vestermarks@svusd.k12.ca.us
Valencia Elementary School
1280 Johnson Avenue
Laguna Hills, CA 92653
Principal: 10 years
School Population: 700 students
Grades: K–6
2004 National Blue Ribbon School of Excellence
2002 California Distinguished School
2000 California Excellence in Arts Education School

Linda Webb
lwebb@austin.isd.tenet.edu
Pillow Elementary School
3025 Crosscreek Drive
Austin, TX 78757
Principal: 4 years
School Population: 404 students
Grades: PreK–5
2004 NCLB Blue Ribbon School
Ms. Webb is currently assistant director of curriculum for the Austin
Independent School District.

Donald Greg Wood
woodgd@spart5.k12.sc.us
Wellford Elementary School
684 Syphrit Road
Wellford, SC 29385
Principal: 10 years
School Population: 570 students
Grades: PreK–3
2003–2004 South Carolina School of Promise
2001–2002 Red Carpet School
2000–2001 Title I Distinguished School
2000–2001 South Carolina Exemplary Writing School

Paul Young
P_young@lancaster.k12.oh.us
West Elementary School
625 Garfield Avenue
Lancaster, OH 43130–2497
Principal: 18 years
School Population: 450 students
Grades: PreK–6
2002–2003 President, National Association of Elementary School
    Principals

Introduction

B ecause I teach in a university educational leadership program, I spend much of my time talking with aspiring principals and other school leaders about the role of the principal in creating effective schools for today's children. Without a doubt, we all agree that the principal is the catalyst for this success or failure. Yet, at the same time, we recognize the difficulty of this important position. Hardly a day goes by that we don't hear at least one of the following concerns about the job of the principal:

- Too stressful
- Too much time is involved and too little time left over for the principal's own family
- Too difficult to satisfy parents and the community
- Too much emphasis on testing
- Too much litigation
- Too difficult to focus on instruction due to societal problems, and, of course,
- Too little pay

In fact, Mertz (1999) reported that principals said the job "involved more work, more pressure and frustration, greater demands, and more responsibilities than even when they assumed the position" (p. 17).

On the other hand, effective principals remind us that this is a job to love. When the role of the principal is successful, principals have rich, fulfilling experiences

- Helping children
- Assisting families
- Supporting teachers
- Strengthening the community
- Contributing to making the world a better place

Toward helping principals have positive experiences, many states have mandated mentor programs, universities have emphasized standards such as NCATE, ISLLC, and ELCC, and countless journal articles, books, and resources have been produced that detail effective practices.

With the goal of contributing to a strong foundation of support for new principals, struggling principals, and principals who are just in need of one more good idea, I began to wonder what principals who have been recognized for being the very best would say when asked about their most important best practices. So I e-mailed, telephoned, and wrote letters to elementary school principals who were recognized for their success as principals. Responses included National Distinguished Principal award winners, principals of Blue Ribbon Schools, and other recognized principals. These award-winning elementary school principals shared many of the "best practices" that have helped build effective elementary schools. Principals who contributed to this book lead public and private schools in a variety of settings throughout the United States. Their schools represent an array of diverse populations in regard to location, socioeconomics, ethnicity, learning styles, and other differences.

Award-winning principals' best practice ideas focused on the following categories:

- Leadership
- Shaping campus culture
- Collaborating and communicating
- Effective instructional programs
- School improvement plans
- At-risk programs

In addition, many of these successful principals added other helpful hints, as well as brief words of wisdom. They also suggested books, which have been compiled in a recommended reading list in Chapter 9.

In addition to learning about best practices, it is also important that principals be reflective. In fact, a valuable activity for principals is to reflect on experiences of the school day every day. It is this process of reflection that contributes to trying out new ideas and affirming or changing processes, programs, and behaviors. Reflection leads to critical self-inspection of personal and professional actions, which leads to self-correction. This is an ongoing process with effective leaders at all levels. As you read through these ideas, reflect on your school. Identify areas where your school is strong. But also identify those areas where there is a need. Which ideas in these chapters would be most helpful to your campus? Write these ideas down; then consider how you can implement them in your school. How might the ideas need to be revised to be effective on your campus? Questions for reflection are provided at the end of each chapter. Also at the end of each chapter, I have included Web sites for some of the programs or concepts mentioned as a quick resource for gathering additional information.

Effective principals are busy people. Their workday starts early in the morning and often ends late at night. Thomas Edison said, "Results! Why, man, I have gotten a lot of results. I know several thousand things that won't work." The best practice ideas in this book work. They have proven to be successful, and this success has led to these schools and their principals being recognized at state and national levels. To the principals who contributed, thank you for sharing your award-winning best practice ideas to help future award-winning principals.

REFERENCE

Mertz, N. (1999). Through their own eyes: Principals look at their jobs. In F. Kochan, B. Jackson, & D. Duke (Eds.), *A thousand voices from the firing line* (pp. 119–139). Columbia, MO: University Council of Educational Administration.

*With loving appreciation to my mother,
who taught me early the value of learning and,
even more, the value of learning from the best.*

and

*To busy school administrators who, despite
the many challenges of their jobs, use their expertise, talents,
and best practice ideas to bring a better tomorrow to children.*

Leadership

A leader is someone who has the capacity to create a compelling vision that takes people to a new place, and to translate that vision into action. Leaders draw other people to them by enrolling them in their vision. What leaders do is inspire people, empower them. They pull rather than push.

—Warren Bennis

There was a time when America's schools were young and principals could be successful by primarily emphasizing good management skills. While these skills remain necessary, the elementary school principal of today is challenged with far-reaching responsibilities that focus on creating a learning organization to enable all children to experience success. This is a huge undertaking and transcends managerial duties to being able to integrate complex leadership behaviors that address student diversity, change processes, a growing knowledge base, technology, personnel decisions, curriculum, and instruction, to name only a few. Joseph Murphy and Amanda Datnow (2003), in *Leadership Lessons From Comprehensive School*

Reform, emphasize a crucial link between principal leadership and successful reform implementation by noting the "importance of a principal in bringing a reform design to the school" (p. 265). In fact, it is only with the principal's leadership vision FOR change and commitment TO change that implementation of an innovation is likely to succeed. It is the leader who creates "the state of mind that is the school" (John W. Gardner, quoted in Blaydes, 2003, p. 141).

When these award-winning principals submitted ideas about leadership in their schools, they emphasized the importance of a shared and purposeful vision. They also noted the importance of creating, nurturing, and sustaining this vision by spending quality time with faculty and students and by drawing a distinction between being a collaborative leader and being a boss. Paul Young even challenges principals to lead by integrating a "show business" approach into much of what we do in our schools. Clearly, for these award-winning principals, leadership is focused around a vision for education that provides an environment where children have every opportunity to be successful and support is maintained for the faculty to lead them in this endeavor.

THE NEED FOR A SHARED VISION

Kim Boelkes
Canton, Illinois

I don't know a dedicated educator anywhere in the nation that doesn't want his or her students to succeed. Yet, one of the most confounding and perplexing challenges we face as educators continues to be why some schools succeed where others fail. Why do some students succeed and others stagnate? In the end, we can look at all of the data, all of the research, and all of the experimentation. We can make excuses or we can make our own judgments and develop our own strategies that will help ensure our success.

Before the judgments, before the strategies and the plans, there must be a vision, a goal. What do you want your students to achieve? How do you define success? Then, and only then, can you decide how you're going to get there and what obstacles you must overcome on the way.

When I began at Eastview Elementary School, there was no clear vision driving our organization. All the staff wanted students to succeed, but many of our students weren't successful. Why? After looking at data, statistics, and teacher performance, we determined it was not due to lack of effort. Our staff worked very hard each day, every day.

We realized teaching methods needed to be changed. We needed to empower our students to learn. No longer could our staff, students, and parents just let education happen. Teachers were using teaching methods that were outdated and obsolete. The staff did what they had done for the past several years—even if it didn't work. Teachers didn't try new teaching methods, because new methods came with too much risk. No one was encouraged to reach beyond the status quo.

Our curriculum wasn't aligned. How could we expect students to score in the "exceeds" category if they were being assessed on a concept they had not been taught? It didn't take a scholar to determine that this approach wasn't working. Faced with this dilemma, and being tired of hanging our heads when test scores were released, we decided to change our future. The futurist Alvin Toffler said several years ago that in the 21st century, the uneducated won't be those who cannot read or write, but those who cannot learn, unlearn, and relearn again. We focused our attention on success. We began with a vision: "To empower all students to succeed in a changing world." We adopted a set of beliefs and a set of values reflective of our learning community and defining in terms of what we wanted for our clients.

Essential to success was the active involvement of our stakeholders—parents, staff, and students. This commitment began to drive our organization. Decisions on spending, staffing issues, and curriculum needed to revolve around our goal. Empowering all students and empowering all parents required us to think differently. Empowerment can either be slick sloganeering or it can be a real change in behavior. We made it the latter. The staff was introduced to the analysis of data. New teaching methods were tried. We embraced and encouraged collaboration and teamwork. Teachers needed to change their teaching to allow students to be empowered in the classroom.

Inservice became part of our everyday life. After allowing our staff the opportunity to spread their wings, we focused on our stakeholders. We invited parents in, fed them, and asked them for help. No longer can schools assume the entire responsibility for learning. All stakeholders must work together to achieve success. Among the beliefs we embraced was that all children could learn. Our challenge became how to find the methods that worked for each student. We embraced the value of encouragement, of positive interaction among administrators, teachers, staff, students, and parents. We committed ourselves to teamwork and mutual respect. If you respect the role each must play in the education process, if you look at yourselves as companions on the same road, then, as the Irish say, the road rises up to greet you. Encouragement breeds like bacteria. The staff feel empowered to teach, students feel empowered to learn, parents feel empowered as citizens and parents.

Education has become a shared responsibility. We fondly call it the 33⅓ rule. Parents, students, and staff each have one-third of the responsibility for education. Each role has no greater or no less value than the others.

H. L. Mencken said that for every human problem, there is a neat, simple solution—and it is always wrong. I know that better than most. I realize these are simple words, that my message is simplistic. The way you implement a vision of empowerment, of stakeholder responsibility, is anything but simple. It is difficult. We have struggled and we are still learning, unlearning, and relearning again, but we are making progress and we believe the risk is worth the reward.

Our goal includes change. This is constant. My vision as an educator has changed drastically over the past 20 years. In 1980, who knew that technology would become a basic teaching tool like the textbook or the chalkboard? What person predicted that our students would have to fear attacks from foreign countries? Who would have thought that it is possible for children to be shot at school? Not I. Adjusting to change means managing change. Don't let it manage you. Revisit your plan each year. Rethink, realign, shift directions if need be and include staff, students, and parents. Don't retreat from your goal or abandon the basic values that form the foundation of your commitment to excellence in education.

CREATING A VISION TO IMPLEMENT YOUR MISSION

Ann Porter
Grand Forks, North Dakota

When I arrived at Lewis & Clark School, the mission statement was a paragraph, something no one knew and much less could remember. At the end of my first year there, I invited five teacher leaders and five parent leaders to a meeting. I asked them to describe Lewis & Clark five years into the future. I wrote their ideas on a *big* piece of paper. It was this exercise that helped us to develop a common vision for our school, to identify our strengths and weaknesses, and to start on a journey together toward that vision.

Also at this meeting, one of the parents asked about our mission statement. Where she worked, everyone could repeat the mission statement. She offered a shortened version of our school's mission: "The mission of the Lewis & Clark School Community is to develop lifelong learners and responsible students." This was shared at staff and parent meetings, as well as in the school's newsletter. Through our school's improvement process, the shortened mission statement was adopted.

The mission statement was posted in every room, including the lunchroom. Every newsletter included the mission statement. At an assembly, I taught the words and their meanings. At our weekly assembly lessons, I introduced students and staff to people who exemplified lifelong learners and responsible citizens. These included veterans, musicians, former students, and civic leaders. These assemblies were opportunities to tell stories of lifelong learners and responsible citizens such as Ben Carlson and Scott O'Grady, whom I had heard at the 2002 NAESP National Convention. When the space shuttle *Columbia* exploded during reentry in October 2003, our next assembly was a solemn one, naming each astronaut and honoring them as lifelong learners and responsible citizens. In the lunchroom, in the hallways, whenever and wherever possible, I would ask students, "Why do you come to school?" They knew! They were becoming lifelong learners and responsible citizens.

As part of our ongoing school improvement process, our mission statement has since been revised to be inclusive. "The mission of the Lewis & Clark School Community is to develop all students into lifelong learners and responsible citizens." It is simple but powerful and meaningful. It is easy to understand and is a grounding influence for all. Our mission statement emphasizes who we want to be.

HAVING A GRAND MISSION

Ramona S. Trevino
Austin, Texas

The story of Zilker Elementary School is a story of academic success within a nested learning community. If there is a common characteristic of excellent principals, I believe it is the ability to inspire, encourage, and set the stage for a school's staff to achieve at high levels. My focus has always been clearly directed toward our ultimate mission: the academic achievement of all. One Zilker teacher said it best by stating, "I have never worked at a school where the mission was as grand and majestic as ours." While Zilker was once a school that often lost students to an affluent neighboring school, it is now the pride of South Austin and the Austin Independent School District, with a waiting list for transfer students.

Qualities of good principal leadership stem from a variety of sources. I am a lead manager who facilitates the decision making on my campus. My career has been greatly impacted by the work of Hank Levin and the Accelerated Schools movement. Three basic philosophies that I continue to articulate and encourage are that of unity of purpose, empowerment coupled with responsibility, and building off strengths. I have encouraged creating systems that help facilitate the communication and decision making of the organization. New mental models were created to address the needs of the school. The highest priority was given to teaching and learning, and a diagnostic prescriptive approach was adopted. Data analysis, campus planning, and parental outreach were keys to our strategic approach to addressing the achievement gap. With a diverse population of 48% White, 46% Hispanic, 6% African American, 50% economically disadvantaged, 17% special education, 15% limited English proficient, and 9% gifted and talented, we had our challenges to address.

Systems thinking identified the need for a clear road map necessary for guiding our school with successful communication. Being an ex–special education teacher, the development of goals and objectives to meet desired outcomes was a concept I embraced. I stressed the importance of the Campus Improvement Plan and the full participation of the staff and community in its development.

An important piece to this development was the analysis of data. Results-based planning soon became an integral part of Campus Advisory Council discussion. I streamlined the process for input in planning by creating a Campus Planning

Packet. This packet, which contained survey results, Academic Excellence Indicator System (AEIS) data, campus data, current campus mission, beliefs, goals, objectives and action steps, and teacher recommendations, went out to all Campus Advisory Council representatives, who received input from represented groups before meeting at a retreat to piece our new plan together. Parent and PTA representatives went out of their way to call special sessions to gather information. Our lengthy annual meeting produced a draft campus plan that went back to groups for review and feedback and later to the Campus Advisory Council for Adoption. Every member of the staff committed to the final draft plan by signing off on it. The plan guided each leadership group represented in the school, including the PTA executive board, team leaders, and Campus Advisory Council. Unity of purpose was established early through this system of planning and has continued to be valued as a high priority.

Other systems of organizing include the development of our yearly calendar. In early summer, I meet with the PTA president and outline a draft calendar of all events, meetings, deadlines, and celebrations. This gives order to our year and paces our work. Meetings involving team leaders, grade-level faculty, vertical teams, technology staff development, student leadership council, Campus Advisory Council, PTA executive board, and community coffees are held on a regular schedule, with agenda items often repeating themselves for full discussion and input from all stakeholders. It is evident at Zilker that whatever the issue our school is facing, there is an appropriate place and time to discuss it openly, gather data, and recommend a solution. This empowers both the staff and parents in decision making. All parties contribute and feel respected in their input into the development of the school. Throughout the organization, procedures and routines have been established to ensure implementation of initiatives and quality performance and results.

A Leadership Action Plan for Improving Practice

Karen Lyon
DeLand, Florida

As head of school, I see myself as a resource, a facilitator, a supporter, and a mentor for the entire St. Barnabas Episcopal School community. In addition, I must be a master diagnostician. The head of school's role necessitates that he or she be able to "diagnose problems" and "analyze available resources and solutions." These tasks require an ability to "read" a school's goals, commitments, context, and resources. Diagnosis requires understanding a school's strengths and weaknesses. It means setting priorities, spurring others to act, and thinking for the long term. Understanding and delivering what the school needs is the leader's core job: *A leader must be concerned with initiating changes in established structures, procedures, or goals.*

Over the past year and a half, I have spent a great deal of time examining my own leadership qualities through prayer and study, visiting other schools, reflecting on best practice, and strategizing ways of initiating change. I looked at both the strengths and weaknesses of my leadership and sought ways to implement change in a positive and motivating way. The priority was to find ways to energize the faculty, bring unity and cohesiveness to interpersonal relationships, and learn new ways of sharing leadership with my peers.

In the April 2004 *Educational Leadership,* Portin identified seven core functions of school leadership in an article titled "The Roles That Principals Play." These roles were the following:

- Instructional leadership: Ensuring quality of instruction, modeling teaching practices, supervising curriculum, and ensuring quality of teaching resources
- Cultural leadership: Tending to the symbolic resources of the school (its traditions, climate, and history)

- Managerial leadership: Overseeing the operations of the school (its budget, schedule, facilities, safety, and security)
- Human resources leadership: Recruiting, hiring, firing, inducting, and mentoring teachers and staff; developing leadership capacity and professional development opportunities
- Strategic leadership: Promoting vision, mission, and goals—and developing a means to reach them
- External development leadership: Representing the school in the community, developing capital, tending to the public relations, recruiting students, buffering and mediating external interests, and advocating for the school's interests
- Micropolitical leadership: Buffering and mediating internal interest while maximizing resources (financial and human)

I practice all of these tenets on a daily, weekly, and yearly basis, but after an in-depth examination of leaders and leadership functions, I concluded that my most effective leadership should be concentrated on developing a yearlong plan to ensure harmony, cooperation, and trust among and between faculty. It was important that I ignite an enthusiasm in them that would foster their internal value of their love of helping others, especially children, to succeed. Graciously accepting our inevitable human interdependency and deliberately nurturing a personal network of supportive others enhance our ability to involve people in our lives in wholesome ways that not only affirm our respect for them and acknowledge their importance to us but also improve the quality of our personal effectiveness. The following vision specifically focuses on instructional and strategic leadership functions.

Last year, I had the opportunity to visit Independent Day School and Dr. Joyce Swarzman, headmistress of the school. She introduced me to strategies that she had used with her faculty and with the Florida Council of Independent School Academies held twice a year at Independent Day School. I chose to follow her lead, and I improvised these strategies to accommodate the corporate needs of my school. I became aware that the faculty needed to input ideas and create a vision for the school. Then they needed to be actively involved in carrying out the vision. The vehicle I chose was the FISH philosophy based on the following books by Lundin, Christensen, and Paul: *FISH!* (2000), *FISH! Tales* (2002), and *FISH! Sticks* (2003).

Pike Place Fish is a world-famous market in Seattle, Washington, that is wildly successful thanks to its fun, bustling, joyful atmosphere and great customer service. Once I read the three books, I knew that I could energize those around me and hopefully effect a transformation among the faculty and staff.

The theme for the 2003–2004 school year has been Vision With Action. The faculty participated in workshops and self-study to develop the vision for the school and in so doing took the required actions to make the vision come into focus. During postplanning (June) and preplanning (August) sessions, the faculty reviewed the videos *Fish* and *The Power of Vision*. Then they broke into small groups and categorized changes or additions they would like to see made in the school's vision. The result of this survey served as the beginning of this year's inservice plan, which is outlined below.

How the Vision With Action Works

General Objectives

1. To develop a schoolwide Vision With Action plan

2. To give the faculty an opportunity to develop their interpersonal relationships

3. To give the faculty methods and skills to more effectively communicate with staff, parents, and students

Specific Objectives

1. The faculty will continue to develop a true vision for the school.

2. The faculty will develop action plans to carry out the vision.

3. The faculty will have an understanding of the FISH philosophy.

4. The faculty will develop real-time actions to carry out and practice the FISH philosophy.

5. The faculty will become more cohesive across grade levels and school levels and buildings (preschool, primary, elementary, and middle school).

6. The faculty will be able to demonstrate techniques for promoting professional behavior, using examples and nonexamples.

7. The faculty will be able to identify strategies for using teacher expectations, the vision of the school, and the FISH philosophy to encourage student achievement.

8. The faculty will be able to identify strategies for using teacher expectations, the vision of the school, and the FISH philosophy to encourage and increase parent support for the school as a whole.

Activities

- The faculty will be reintroduced to the vision precepts.
- Vision is emotionally charged and intellectually challenging to produce.
- A vision is a picture we can see with the mind's eye.
- A vision engages your heart and spirit.
- A vision taps into embedded concerns and needs.
- A vision asserts what you and your colleagues want.
- A vision provides meaning to the work you and your colleagues do.
- A vision is simple but not always clear.
- A vision is a living document that can always be expanded.
- A vision provides a starting place from which to get to more and more levels of specificity.
- A vision is based on two deep human needs: quality and dedication.

1. The faculty will be reintroduced to the FISH philosophy:

    a. **Choose Your Attitude:** You have the privilege of choosing your attitude each day. "When you are doing what you are doing, who are you being? Are you being impatient and bored, or are you being world famous? You are going to act differently if you are being world famous." Who do we want to be while we do our work?

    b. **Play:** Fun is energizing. You must have fun while you work. How could we have more fun and create more energy? You have a choice: whistle while you work, sling FISH, or whatever other fun and creative ideas you come up with.

    c. **Make Their Day:** It is important to include your customers in the good time. Engage the customers in ways that create energy and goodwill. Our customers are the students, parents, grandparents, friends of the school, the community at large, and yes, even ourselves. How can we engage them in a way that will make their day? How can we make each others' days?

    d. **Be Present:** Be fully present at work. What can the FISH guys teach us about being present for each other and our customers?

2. The faculty will be divided into four groups (heterogeneous groups across grade levels) matching the four components of the FISH philosophy (Choose Your Attitude, Play, Make Their Day, Be Present), and in a group over the period of six weeks, with a budget of $100 per group, they will study and develop an action plan in their particular component of the FISH philosophy and show how it relates to their everyday personal lives and to school.

3. In October, the teachers developed professional goals for the year around the four precepts of the FISH philosophy. They developed these guided by the following questions:

     a. How can you integrate the FISH precepts into your personal life?

     b. How can you professionally integrate the FISH precepts?

     c. What are the three or four ways you can bring the FISH precepts into the classroom for your students?

4. The individual groups made a presentation to the faculty, including a positive action plan that the entire faculty could incorporate into their daily lives.

5. Each group made a presentation to the entire faculty about their part of the philosophy and how it is brought into their daily lives at school. They incorporated real-time activities that could be done by all on a daily basis. All activities were guided and grounded by scripture chosen by the St. Barnabas School Prayer Group. These scriptures were titled *Fish Philosophy From the Ultimate Fisherman.*

6. Using the Master Teacher Literature Program, the study groups continued after Christmas to study individual topics and present salient information to the entire faculty, giving examples of how to incorporate the information and suggestions into their daily classroom setting. This was done through a PowerPoint presentation. These were the topics chosen:

     a. Tapping the Instructional Power of Symbolic Thinking

     b. Eight Guidelines for Keeping Class Discussions Moving

     c. Secrets of Teaching That Your Students Want You to Know

     d. Seven Commandments for Communicating With Parents

     e. Creating Lesson Plans That Work Every Time

     f. How the Arts Impact Learning in Your Classroom

   g. Six Ways to Help Students Remember What They've Learned

   h. Six Daily Actions That Motivate Students to Learn

7. The final activity was to have peer evaluations. Cross-grade-level teachers were selected to evaluate a lesson that was based on Bloom's Taxonomy and the theory of multiple intelligences. As part of this evaluation, the teachers were to meet for a preconference before the observation and a postconference after the observation. The evaluator was to also complete a Multiple Intelligences Environment checklist, which helps to verify that all intelligences are represented in the classroom environment. The teacher being observed was to also fill out a teacher reflection inventory, which was shared with the peer evaluator during the postconference.

Evaluation

1. Each teacher has had an opportunity to look at himself or herself and develop individual goals for the 2004–2005 school year based on the conferences, teacher reflection inventory, Bloom's Taxonomy, theory of multiple intelligences, and the FISH philosophy. Each teacher has met with the administration reviewing the evaluation and discussing the goals for the upcoming school year.

2. At the postteaching, the faculty will present the vision, identifying ways the school's vision can be expanded and enhanced by the action plans presented by the faculty.

3. A plan will be formulated by teachers and administration to create a road map showing the extension of the vision to the next level.

4. Strategies will be developed to keep the FISH philosophy alive in the coming years, with the ultimate goal of keeping morale and unity among the faculty at high levels.

5. *Quantum Teaching: Orchestrating Student Success* by DePorter, Reardon, and Singer-Nourie (1999) will be assigned to all the teachers as a summer read. The faculty will participate in reading groups during the next school year to develop teaching strategies that can be applied in the classroom.

The goal of leadership is to create an idea and present the idea in such a way that the participants are inspired and motivated by unity of purpose and mutually shared values. I believe that this has been a pivotal year of study that has been inspirational for the entire staff. We have been transformed to live in a workplace that is filled with energy and enthusiasm. Our schoolwide philosophy has become "As you enter this place of work, please choose to make today a great day. Your colleagues, customers, team members, and you yourself will be thankful. Find ways to play. We can be serious about our work without being serious about ourselves. Stay focused in order to be present when your customers and team members most need you. And should you feel your energy lapsing, try this surefire remedy: Find someone who needs a helping hand, a word of support, or a good ear—and make their day."

In Stephen Covey's book *The 7 Habits of Highly Effective People* (1995), he outlines strategies to help individuals realize their full potential. The seventh habit is "sharpening the saw," which includes taking time for study, reflection, goal setting, and retooling. This is very important for administrators, as so much of the job is consumed by day-to-day responsibilities and reacting to minicrises. It is important to take time periodically to take advantage of professional development opportunities, visit other schools to collaborate with peers, and study and reflect on best practices. These opportunities enable all of us to be better leaders.

Most leaders want to accomplish goals that matter, inspire others to join them in working toward these goals, and leave a legacy after they have gone. I believe that important life-changing goals have been accomplished this year, and I am proud of and love the outstanding faculty and staff at

St. Barnabas Episcopal School. The administration has full confidence that there is a true vision, purpose, and meaning that has been developed this year and that we are entering the future with a solid foundation that is undergirded by love, mutual trust, and prayer.

A Vision for Immersion Language Education: Becoming Bilingual

Ursina Swanson
St. Louis Park, Minnesota

At Park Spanish Immersion School, we believe that elementary schools benefit greatly from having a clear, strong focus and vision. Our school is unique in that, as a public school of choice, we teach the entire curriculum in Spanish, beginning with the first day of kindergarten. Only in second and third grade do we begin some minimal formal English language instruction. Spanish is used as the vehicle to teach course content. Families come to our school because they wish their children to be bilingual. They value global education, and they want their children to gain an understanding of other cultures and to be taught in this unique and innovative educational setting. In fact, because our students, most of whom are from English-speaking homes, learn the language at such a young age, their accent and intonation in Spanish is flawless and thoroughly nativelike. The school has become increasingly well established and known. Many parents who want to enroll their children in our school are unable to do so; because of this, PSI has been obligated to establish a lottery system for selecting incoming students.

The mission of PSI is to "provide bilingual education which promotes academic excellence, intellectual curiosity and cultural understanding. The school involves family and community in the development of lifelong learners who hold themselves and others in the highest regard." Everyone on our staff supports this goal of Spanish language acquisition. This includes our secretaries and custodians, who also support this mission to the best of their ability. For example, though our secretary is not completely bilingual, she does know many Spanish phrases and uses these whenever she has the opportunity to do so. All PSI staff are focused on the same objectives. It is the principal's role to continuously hold forth this mission and vision to the staff.

Academics, of course, are just as important at our school as at other public schools. In Minnesota, the Minnesota Comprehensive Assessment (MCA) is given in the third and fifth grades at the elementary level. Consistently, our immersion students have attained some of the highest scores in the state, even though the test is given in English and the students have learned all their lessons in Spanish.

Even though we teach the entire curriculum in Spanish, we also offer solid English language instruction beginning in the third grade. At PSI we do not have a longer school day than other schools, even though we teach a dual curriculum. In order to gain time, teachers are encouraged to integrate what has been learned in Spanish during English instruction. For example, when teaching punctuation in English Language Arts, students are reminded about what they learned in the Spanish Language Arts class and that punctuation rules are almost the same in English. This teaches children in the early elementary years to look closely at language and to recognize the parallels that exist between languages. Another time enhancement that we support is to ask our parents to commit to reading to their children daily in English at home.

Behavioral and discipline issues are another area where we are careful not to waste time. To help us with this, all staff integrate Responsive Classroom principles into the classroom and school day. (Responsive Classroom is a practical approach to creating safe, challenging, and joyful elementary schools.) This helps students acquire social skills, which support their academic learning. When students have clear expectations and guidelines to follow, there is less time spent on behavioral management and more time spent on teaching and learning.

The premise of Responsive Classroom is that social development is as important as the academic development of the child. We guide children throughout the day in this balanced approach to learning. We also believe that how children learn is as important as what they learn. Therefore, students are given parameters in learning to be responsible citizens. For example, we emphasize self-control by encouraging and supporting students to behave in an ethical way. When students do not act responsibly, there are logical and clear consequences, such as time-out or restitution. It is important that these are implemented in a clear, consistent manner.

One challenge at PSI is to find faculty who are nativelike or native speakers of Spanish. I spend much energy and time in recruiting qualified teachers throughout the year who must pass a stringent Spanish language assessment that we give. Minnesota state law requires that all teachers have a Minnesota teaching license. This means that I must work closely with new faculty to help them earn this state teaching license. Furthermore, it is important that the principal leading a language immersion school have foreign language skills, particularly in the language being taught. As a French speaker, I have made ongoing efforts to acquire Spanish language communication skills myself.

In leading our school, I emphasize the importance of building cultural appreciation. In fact, it is through the learning of another language that an appreciation of other cultures is made possible. Our faculty represents 14 different nationalities from Latin America and Europe. As students learn the language, they also acquire strong cultural competencies.

Purposeful Leadership

John Ciesluk
Longmeadow, Massachusetts

Principals articulate and instill in others a strong sense of purpose. Their vigorous pursuit of sound educational values and goals elevates the status of their schools and moves others closer to fulfilling their schools' missions.

We have a motto at Wolf Swamp Road Elementary School: "Eyes on the child learning." This motto guides decisions the school makes as it considers new initiatives. During the past three years, learning about the Baldrige Framework for Continuous Improvement has added resonance to this phrase. It has truly led to a continuous improvement culture in which all practices are reviewed on a regular basis using a PDSA (Plan, Do, Study, Act) cycle. A teacher study group meets monthly to ensure that the Baldrige efforts are refined and best practices are documented in a three-ring binder. Through the three years of Baldrige work, staff and students have moved to new levels as lifelong learners. They are committed to high expectations for all, and schoolwide alignment is emerging in a variety of ways.

A first step toward improvement was the revision of the school's mission statement. All staff participated in the development of a new mission statement: "To provide a safe, caring, respectful learning community that encourages every child to achieve at his or her full potential."

In addition, teachers translated the three school improvement objectives into "kid-friendly" terms. The mission and improvement objectives are posted for all to see, and students, as well as teachers, are expected to articulate what they will do to advance the objectives. Students demonstrate greater understanding of learning expectations, develop their own learning plans based on the school's objectives, and self-assess their progress on a weekly basis. Students are working harder and learning more.

Regular communication to parents documents work on the improvement targets, and parental input is solicited regarding the school's success in addressing them. In addition, even the custodial staff has surveyed the staff to see what they can do to better address the school's mission.

Quality Time With Staff

Gloria L. Kumagai
St. Paul, Minnesota

Our school, Museum Magnet Elementary School, has a diverse population, with 33% of our children African American, 33% Asian American, and 33% White. In addition, 59% of our children are on a free or reduced lunch plan.

Every year, at the beginning of the new school year, I meet with all of our staff individually. At this meeting, we identify individual and professional goals for the new school year and different ways that these goals can be met. From this meeting, I am able to assess staff strengths and interests so that appropriate mentoring, resources, and opportunities can be offered to them during the year. Then at the end of the school year, we meet again with each staff person to revisit these goals and review how they were accomplished.

Another especially helpful way that we have quality staff time is through a team-building exercise that I use during our staff development days. For this activity, we form a circle beginning with the person who has been at the school the longest and ends with the newest staff member. The first question each person answers is, Why did you come to this school? The second question is, Why do you stay? The last question is, What do you have to offer? By participating in this activity, staff members are able to see similarities and differences between themselves, and at the same time, passion for and commitment to the school are reflected.

Examining data is also a part of the quality time that I spend with faculty. At the beginning of each school year, teachers examine the previous spring's test results to analyze baseline data. This includes disaggregated data for each of the students in our school. Using this information, teachers develop a plan describing how they will strengthen areas of weakness. Then teachers meet with me individually to review the plan to ensure that they have resources, both human and material, to assist with implementation. We also have an ongoing assessment when teachers assess students every six to eight weeks so that their instruction is directed all the time at student instructional levels. Then I meet with teachers throughout the year so that we are continually assessing student progress and allocation of resources.

NOT THE BOSS . . . THE LEADER

Exerta T. Mackie
Houston, Texas

In John Maxwell's book *Developing the Leader Within You* (1993, pp. 5–6), he emphasizes the differences between a leader and a boss. The boss says "I" and blames others when things break down, but a leader says "we" and helps correct what breaks down. While the boss may *know* how something is done, a leader *shows* how it is done. These are some of the concepts that have inspired and governed my leadership method. I operate on the premise of being a leader rather than a boss, and this principle has manifested itself in the staff members that I lead. My key role as a leader is to chart a course and provide directions to those I lead. The principal is at the core of everything that goes on in the school and provides the vision and lays out the expectations of the school. He or she must then practice the right blend of management and human relations to get the job done. The idea is to get the staff to do the job and enjoy it at the same time. Effective school leaders must operate on the belief of enabling staff members to actuate campus improvement. The principal, the instructional leader of the school, progressively empowers staff by letting them share in the decision-making process.

I firmly believe that principals must concern themselves with controlling the conditions that enable employees to function in ways that will increase the likelihood that shared goals will be realized, rather than controlling what they do and how they do it. It is this empowerment of staff that creates increased self-confidence and leads to new perspectives on what works to improve teaching and learning.

I perceive the school as a learning organization not for students only but for all staff members, parents, and the community as well. Successful leaders are perpetual learners and have the ability to instill in others the desire to learn what is necessary to help the organization to reach its mission. The leader must model for all within the workplace what lifelong learning means.

Triumphant principals are effective managers. They listen, communicate, and develop relationships with staff, students, parents, and other stakeholders connected to the school and its operation. As managers, it is critical to display respect for every individual who contributes to the success of the school. Principals must always remember that some employees may appear to be on the periphery, but everyone involved contributes in his or her own way to the school's success. In sum, successful principals lead by example and model expectations.

RESPECT FOR ALL

Gina Segobiano
Belleville, Illinois

All good administrators make an effort to get to know each and every faculty and staff member on a professional basis as well as on a personal basis. It shouldn't matter if you are a teacher or a crossing guard—the principal must strive to build positive relationships with all school employees. Developing sincere and supportive relationships is essential to maintaining positive morale and establishing an educational climate that is one of mutual respect and appreciation. Teachers and staff members need to know that you not only care about them but that you take a special interest in them, regardless of their position.

Take a look at your relationships with your building staff. Do you know everyone's name? Make sure you know at least three important things about each employee: spouse or significant other's name? Kids' names? A sports fan? A runner? A cook? A traveler? A scrapbook fanatic? Engage in meaningful conversations that focus on personal interests and recognize accomplishments made by your employees and their families. Make a special note to congratulate a teacher's husband who just retired or post a newspaper article featuring one of your teacher's kids in the sports section. It is okay to not talk about educational topics all the time. Share with your staff personal interests of your own. Everyone on my staff knows my husband, my kids, my unhealthy eating habits, my excessive attendance at soccer games, and my getaways to the lake. By the way, it is also okay to attend an afterschool social with the faculty once in a while. You need to know your staff as individuals, just as they need to know you as an individual. Just make sure you are not the last to leave!

Aside from building professional and personal relationships with all staff members, every administrator should fully understand the job duties of all employees and, when needed, fill in when necessary. By lending a helping hand in a time of need, the principal sets a good example for all the students by showing them that the principal is not "too good" to perform the job duties of any staff member in the building. In addition, your staff members appreciate the help. By performing the duties of all staff members, the principal engages in conversation with surrounding employees, students, and parents—again, building relationships with all stakeholders.

If you are the principal, you have not fulfilled your responsibility unless you have done the following: served food in the cafeteria, filled in for the crossing guard at the busiest intersection at dismissal, answered phones in the office, checked out books for the kindergarteners in the library and put back library books on the shelves, cleaned up a wet spill in the hallway (by the time a custodian could have arrived on the scene, the mess would already be cleaned!), checked for lice (that is not my favorite), monitored the playground, set up 200 chairs for the PTO meeting, picked up litter on school grounds, and my favorite: directed the school band! Immerse yourself! Get to know all employees and all job duties! You might have fun!

LEADERSHIP BY SHOW BUSINESS: IT'S TIME FOR "SHOW BUSINESS" TO REPLACE "SHOW AND TELL"

Paul Young
Lancaster, Ohio

Like the well-worn elementary school activity, many education practices simply show and tell our customers, the public, often lacking any significant human interaction or emotional connection. Instead, the business of education could be dramatically improved by integrating a show business approach into much of what we do.

What Scott McLain suggests to business leaders in his book *All Business Is Show Business* is also applicable for educational leaders. Most people working in the field of education would assume that their business is focused on teaching, learning, or providing some related support service. But what we must learn is that the real business of education is that of creating relationships and emotional connections with people: students, staff, parents, and the diverse members of the community. When that focus is mastered, our customers (the public, including students) know that someone cares for them, they are treated with respect, and the positive experiences and interactions lead to improved service, teaching, and learning. Good teachers have always known this. It is time that we let all school employees, from all levels of the organization, in on the secrets. And what are those secrets? Nothing novel—just good common sense and concern for people, which successful businesses have mastered for years.

McLain uses a simple example and points out that for over 30 years, children have been taught their ABC's by Big Bird, Bert, and Ernie. Consequently, when they come to school, even on their very first day, they expect to be entertained while they are being educated. Principals see this being played out in classrooms every day. Where teachers can hold students' attention by entertaining, developing personal, emotional connections with their students, student attendance, behavior, and achievement are often higher. Where the classroom environment is blah and boring, students don't take long to show and tell their lack of interest. Whether we choose to acknowledge this phenomenon or not, this is the reality of schools.

High-stakes testing has driven school personnel to focus on standards, realign curriculum, and teach to the tests. Resulting test data are often disappointing. Yet, there are many shining examples of master teachers (performers in the classroom) who instinctively connect with diverse learners, overcome the odds, and achieve success. The study of these relationships, and how they can be implemented throughout all levels of the school business, can lead to the high level of performance the public expects and demands.

Educators often cringe when business practices are cited as improvement models for schools. But a show business philosophy is far different from the typical models of business of the corporate world. The purpose of school show business is to create emotional connections that are so satisfying to customers and employees that loyalty is ensured. Moreover, it will work and produce results, and it won't add to already strapped budgets. Some simple tenets of the show business philosophy, focused on product, service, and experience, can be implemented everywhere.

For the Public

1. Enable customers to connect with the product: teaching and learning. It must be of the highest caliber.

2. Focus on human emotional connections and experiences. These experiences must be satisfying to the customer. Employ receptionists or greeters (even volunteers) at all levels of the organization.

3. Meet the needs of the customers, whatever it takes.

4. Provide the public with a story they can tell others. The story will stick in their minds far longer than a list of facts and data.

For Students

1. Teachers must emulate strategies of entertainers; students have continuous exposure to these strategies in their real world.

2. Focus less on the technical aspects of mastery of information and more on the mastery of teacher-student interactions. Develop a personal, emotional connection with each student, no matter the size of the classroom or school.

3. Prepare for each lesson as an actor does before going on stage.

4. Provide service to all students that meets needs and extends beyond the classroom.

For Employees

1. Employees are the show business of schools from the public's point of view. They are the school. Invest what it takes to make employees loyal to the organization so they will create amazing emotional connections with customers.

2. Enable all employees to feel important, valued, and a part of the team. Encourage social interactions.

3. Provide professional growth opportunities and networking within and outside the organization.

4. Continuously develop strategies that enable employees to enhance their abilities to perform their jobs.

As school personnel meet the requirements of No Child Left Behind, IDEA and other federal, state, and district mandates and expectations, working harder at an old plan will likely produce many of the same results. A different, bold new plan is needed. The answer is right in front of us. We have almost 24-7 exposure to opportunities. Perception is reality. If our customers perceive we are blah, boring, and failing to meet their needs—we are!

Let's learn what many already know. Let's get past our traditional show-and-tell attitudes and determine that the business of education, in every aspect and level, will be dramatically improved when we are all "on stage" and create experiences and service that will "wow" the public.

SNAPSHOTS

Leadership by Being Visible

Robert W. Fowls
Bend, Oregon

During my weekly planning, I intentionally block out periods of time when I personally wander around the school visiting classrooms, labs, playgrounds, and hallways. I made a point of always speaking with the children, and many times I just give out a bunch of hugs, which helps them feel comfortable with their administrator. The teachers appreciate my visibility, since it goes a long way in supporting the positive climate of our school.

Lots of Leaders

Marla W. McGhee
Austin, Texas

Our campus developed *lots* of leaders among the staff and parent community (assistant principals, principals, and teacher leaders). Some of these folks have gone on to become renowned staff developers, lawyers, experts in various educational fields, instructors in teacher education programs or alternative certification of teacher programs, university instructors, and doctoral candidates. We accomplished this through strong and steadfast collaboration and support. This even meant occasionally nudging people past their comfort zone and telling them they could do it, even when they felt they could not go on or wanted to quit. Then we fully celebrated their accomplishments!

Leading Change on a Campus

Elizabeth Neale
Pittsfield, Massachusetts

Rarely do new principals get assigned to a perfect school. Principals have a window of opportunity within the first 18 months to make serious changes on a campus regarding cultural shifts, faculty thinking, and so on. After all, when a new principal comes to a campus, people are expecting changes. Do lots of consultation and listening, then jump in and make changes. If you wait too long, it becomes harder to bring about change. In fact, a sense of complacency sets in and it is harder for everyone, including you, the principal, to address needed changes.

Leadership Direction

Dawn Smith
Warm Springs, Oregon

Leadership in a building, especially a building undergoing change, moves along a continuum—from very directive at the beginning of the process to a shared leadership model once positive results begin to become apparent. It's critical, then, that principals be knowledgeable about their school communities and be able to identify and articulate areas of need. They must also be able to clearly articulate and model the vision for the school—especially during the first year or two—until everyone in the school community is on board with the vision, goals, and direction of the school. The building leader creates the momentum, pulling everything together and setting the direction while developing the leadership team within the building—those master teachers and parents or community members who understand the building needs and goals—and then begins stepping more into the role of securing the resources the team determines are needed to keep the process moving in the right direction.

I have been able to use the reservation media (tribal newspaper, radio station) from the beginning of our school's change process to talk about our vision and direction for our school and keep community members updated along the way. I also take advantage of every speaking opportunity that comes my way, both within and without the community, to talk about what we are doing, where we are headed, and how we plan on getting there. Once we went to the shared leadership model, teachers, parents, and community members began taking on that "visible" role within the school and district, in the community, and as they traveled to conferences and gatherings throughout the state.

LEADERSHIP REFLECTION

1. Where is my leadership strong?
2. What are leadership needs at my school?
3. Does the school community have a shared vision for our school?
4. What am I doing now to promote a shared vision?
5. What ideas in this chapter will be helpful to strengthen our commitment to a shared vision?
6. Which ideas in this chapter do I especially like?
7. How can we implement these ideas in our school?
8. How might these ideas need to be revised to be successful at our school?

ADDITIONAL RESOURCES

Accelerated Schools movement
http://www.acceleratedschools.net

Baldrige Framework for Continuous Improvement
http://www.quality.nist.gov

Bloom's Taxonomy
http://www.ops.org/reading/blooms_taxonomy.html

Multiple Intelligences
http://www.newhorizons.org/strategies/mi/front_mi.htm

Responsive Classroom
http://www.responsiveclassroom.org

REFERENCES

Blaydes, W. (2003). *The educator's book of quotes.* Thousand Oaks, CA: Corwin.

Covey, S. (1995). *The 7 habits of highly effective people.* New York: St. Martin's Griffin.

Lundin, S., Christensen, J., & Paul, H. (2000). *FISH! A remarkable way to boost morale and improve results.* New York: Hyperion.

Lundin, S., Christensen, J., & Paul, H. (2002). *FISH! tales: Bite-sized stories: Unlimited possibilities.* New York: Hyperion.

Lundin, S., Christensen, J., & Paul, H. (2003). *FISH! sticks.* New York: Hyperion.

Maxwell, J. (1993). *Developing the leader within you.* Nashville, TN: Thomas Nelson.

McLain, S. (2002). *All business is show business.* Nashville, TN: Rutledge Hill Press.

Murphy, J., & Datnow, A. (Eds.). (2003). *Leadership lessons from comprehensive school reform.* Thousand Oaks, CA: Corwin.

Shaping Campus Culture

If I ran a school, I'd give the average grade to the ones who gave me all the right answers, for being good parrots. I'd give the top grades to those who made a lot of mistakes and told me about them, and then told me what they learned from them.

—R. Buckminster Fuller

The culture of the school captures the school's atmosphere and gives it a unique identity. The climate, closely related to the culture of the school, refers to patterns of behavior that manifest the culture. Principals are key leaders in maintaining and changing school cultures. In fact, principals cannot effectively shape a successful school culture unless they understand the culture as it exists in the school and have a vision for what it should be. Thus, successful principals understand the importance of change processes directed at the school climate in order to shape the campus culture effectively. This means that principals must be able to nurture and maintain what is working and be willing and able to revise what is not working.

In shaping and establishing a campus culture that is positive for students, faculty, and the larger community, award-winning principals must have a plan and they must listen to their constituents. Principals in this chapter emphasize the schoolwide nature of the activities that occur on a campus to shape the culture of the school. When instruction, language, procedures, and the many other activities of the school are in harmony with the school's vision and are nurtured by leadership, the climate is one that encourages success for all. Principals must meet the challenge to identify the best from each faculty member and spread this throughout the campus. This chapter begins with a description of a nurturing school day by Scott Hollinger. This is followed by other award-winning principals who describe their best practices to create a positive school culture that include supporting student learning, greeting the day, positive relationships, providing a calm school environment, building a positive school climate, and even serving muffins and donuts.

A Nurturing Place Called School

Scott Hollinger
McAllen, Texas

Life begins early at McAuliffe Elementary School. Although classes won't begin until 8:00 a.m., our cooks have been here since 5:30. The first teacher arrived at 6:55. As the sun rises, custodian César Rodríguez raises the American flag. Our school awakens to another busy day. Soon the cafeteria will be filled with children and parents (breakfast and lunch are free for all students). A line of cars begins to form on North 29th Street passing signs that read DON'T FORGET ICE CREAM MONEY and KISS GOOD-BYE HERE. In the driveway, teachers open car doors, help students out, shake their hands, and welcome them to school. As principal, I shake hands with students, teachers, and parents as they enter the gym. Adults and students are clustering in the gym, shaking hands. (Does everyone shake hands here?)

Music calls stragglers to the gym. The national anthem plays. Nearly a thousand voices say the pledge of allegiance and sing the Native American melody "My Paddle, Clean and Bright" in a four-part round with ostinato. Everyone sings "Happy Birthday" to Alejandra and Alani, and we all repeat the steps of the social skill of following instructions. By 8:00, teachers are leading their students inside the main school building to the strains of "You Are My Sunshine." This morning, we have with us three student teachers from the University of Texas–Pan American, several practicum students from South Texas Community College, and four high school seniors from the South Texas Independent School District (ISD) Business, Education, and Technology Academy. Guests are welcome here; they help define our school community.

Today, four teachers from La Joya ISD will visit with kindergarten teachers Dina Serda and Gaby Morquin about two-way bilingual education. At McAuliffe, we are refining our dual language program, and we expect to learn as much from the La Joya teachers as they'll learn from us. After lunch, teacher Norma Vogel will visit Rayburn Elementary to mentor their new fifth grade Gifted and Talented program teacher. During a time that we call TALL time (Teachers as Lifelong Learners), our third grade teachers will meet with Garland Linkenhoger, our district's math coordinator, to analyze our scores on last year's state exams. This afternoon, two university students will have coffee with first grade teacher Nancy Birkenmayer. Nancy is a contributing author for *Introduction to Early Childhood Education* (Brewer, 1998) and a major author of our district's kindergarten curriculum. At 3:30 in the conference room, counselor Mike Fleischmann will lead 8 colleagues in a study of Ernest L. Boyer's *The Basic School*, while in the library, facilitator Ellie Jazinski will lead 12 others in a discussion of Lucy Calkins's *The Art of Teaching Writing*. At 4:00, multiage teacher Karen Kinerk will go to Memorial High School to attend a faculty meeting of the Regional School for the Deaf. Karen is not a teacher of the deaf, but she has two Rochester School for Deaf students in her class. She'll be attending sign language class later this evening.

Since McAuliffe was born in 1986, our teachers have committed to forging an excellent school. In 1993, we joined the Texas Mentor School Network. Serving as a mentor school is fulfilling for us because we believe as passionately in developing our profession as we believe in developing children. Peer tutoring is not for kids only. To mentor other teachers is to extend our successful practices to other children throughout the state.

As a mentor school, we have helped organize annual mentor conferences in our region. Our teachers have presented at these and other state and national conferences. Our faculty helped write and pilot the state's teacher appraisal instrument, the only school in the Rio Grande Valley to do so.

Teaching others helps to solidify our own learning. As principal I consider myself the lead teacher and have the opportunity to guide more by inspiration than by directive. I love to talk about teaching and learning, and I view the role of the principal as a teacher of teachers.

At 6:30 this evening, teacher Heather Kester will meet with a group of eight parents who will be attending Capturing Kids' Hearts this semester. At 7:30 p.m., Cub Scout Pack 55 will hold their monthly meeting in the cafeteria. At 9:30, we'll begin to turn off the outside lights; at 12:30 a.m., the custodians will call it a night. Tomorrow's a busy day.

SUPPORTING STUDENT LEARNING IN A POSITIVE SCHOOL CULTURE

Lori Musser
Joplin, Missouri

Columbia Elementary School maintains a collaborative and positive school culture that focuses on supporting our students' learning and fosters a caring and compassionate school community. The faculty and staff are committed to using the best practices in their classroom to ensure student success. All decisions made at Columbia are based on the best interests of our students.

A shared decision-making approach is utilized in our school to allow all teachers to have a stake in the decisions that affect our students and our school. Decisions are made based on what is best for our students, and ideas are shared. The old saying "two heads are better than one" is the premise behind our shared decision making.

Teachers at Columbia work diligently to provide effective instruction, focusing on our curriculum objectives. We work together as a cohesive unit sharing ideas, strategies, and resources to improve our students' performance and achievement. Our teachers have attended many professional development activities that are based in research on effective teaching strategies and on children's learning styles. The teachers then implement what they learn in their classrooms. A variety of positive changes and initiatives have occurred at Columbia based on these professional development opportunities. The teachers collaborated to increase instructional time in the areas of communication arts and math in an effort to improve student achievement. Our teachers worked closely to implement the literacy initiatives that include the Early Literacy Program, Reading Recovery, Literacy Wall, and Literacy Team meetings. The Four-Block Approach to teaching reading and the adoption of a new reading series arose out of our teachers' commitment to improving instruction. (Four-Block Reading has four components: Guided Reading, Self-Selected Reading, Writing, and Working with Words.)

Our teachers spend time after school in school improvement meetings discussing school issues and concerns. Through shared decision making and teamwork, Columbia has developed and implemented several new programs to solve problems and promote a positive culture within our school. Programs such as Mustang Mediation, the Life Skills Wall, Math Club, Student Council, and Tutoring were all ideas and initiatives that arose out of Columbia school improvement meetings. These programs were designed specifically and solely to address student issues and to reach our goal of higher achievement. Action research is involved in the implementation of these programs as we continuously assess the successfulness of the outcomes and make revisions as needed.

At Columbia, we realize that we cannot reach our goals alone. We must have the support and involvement of our community and parents. At Columbia, we do have that needed support and continually look for ways to improve it. The positive relationship between school, home, and community is promoted in a variety of ways. Newsletters, daily communication with parents, conferences, phone calls, home visits, and involving parents and community members in our instruction through utilizing volunteers, tutoring, and collaborative efforts are all necessary for our students to achieve. Columbia's teachers serve on many building-level and district-level committees, further illustrating their dedication to our students and improving their instruction. Our teachers attend faculty, grade-level, department, and school improvement meetings. At these meetings, our teachers share the responsibility of making decisions to improve learning for Columbia students.

The faculty and staff at Columbia work together as a cohesive team. Whether a cook, teacher, or engineer, our goal is to provide an environment that helps all the children feel good about themselves. The good of our students' development is always the driving force behind any decisions that are made and are in accordance with our vision statement.

∾

GREET THE DAY!

Ann Porter
Grand Forks, North Dakota

One of my favorite times was the start of each new school day. When I arrived, the halls were silent and dark. I walked the halls, turning on the lights, unlocking teachers' doors, and turning on music from a boom box in each hallway. The school would slowly come alive with early arriving staff and students. I was there to welcome the students to help them learn the morning procedures for hanging up their backpacks and coats, then moving on to breakfast, library, or quiet room, and to check out how their day had started. I would touch base with staff members about a meeting they had attended, how a mother in the hospital was doing, or setting a time for a supervisory meeting. I carried a notepad and pen to write a note to a teacher about his bulletin board. I would see the nurse about a child with a persistent cough or notice a student who needed mittens and boots. One year, I went outside and walked with students. It gave me the opportunity to have informal conversations and model appropriate seasonal dress for students and appropriate supervisory behavior for teachers.

When I became a principal, our schools did not have breakfast or before-school programs. Today's new programs serve parents by providing a safe and welcoming place for their children in the morning, provide time for me to interact with the entire school community, and eliminate many problems we used to have outside the school building with students waiting for our doors to open. Our school district also increased teacher-pupil contact time by starting the school day at 8:10 a.m. instead of 8:45 a.m. without increasing the teachers' contract time. Thus, there was little time for before-school meetings. I didn't miss those meetings! The time spent roaming the school, checking in with students, staff, and parents, was much more valuable for setting a positive tone for teaching and learning.

When I asked my counselor what he considered to be one of my best practices, he said, "You are very present with kids. You set up door duty for staff and role modeled for us as to being present, friendly, and involved with kids and their parents. This is a small thing but a powerful tone setter for the school staff, kids' parents, and kids."

THE SCHOOL ENVIRONMENT

Stephany Bourne
Ft. Wayne, Indiana

In order to focus on learning, the school environment should be calm, quiet, and focused on learning. We were able to accomplish this through the following:

- We implemented a uniform policy. The students wear uniforms every day of the school year except on the last Friday of each month, which is Popcorn Day. On this day, they dress in school spirit wear (T-shirts with our school logo).
- All students recite a peace pledge every morning during announcements and are taught to use conflict resolution as a means of resolving conflicts on the playground and around the building. We have very few referrals and have not had a playground referral for years.
- All students have an academic goal based on a standard. On a random basis, they are asked to recite their goals and give an example.
- There is no downtime at our school. Around the drinking fountains there are vocabulary words to memorize. There are wipe-off boards with "brain challenges" in the halls. When I ride the school buses throughout the year, we have an "academic ride." All students are quietly doing homework.
- Everything we do here is about making good or poor choices. Once the culture is established, students strive to make good choices and are proud when they react to a bad choice appropriately.
- Our school is good about connecting with parents on a regular basis when a student makes a poor choice.
- Forming a team to address poor behaviors has been very successful. Our top priority is to curb bullying. We

get few reports of students making fun of others. Our school works on this continuously through various modes to stamp out teasing.

RELATIONSHIPS ARE KEY

Linda Webb
Austin, Texas

I believe the success of students is reliant upon the relationships within the school. You must first and foremost create a common vision for school based on the students' needs, and all of your actions must be seen as aligned to that vision. The relationship of the adult learners (teachers, administrators, and parents) must be one of trust. Building trust takes time, but your investment will reap great benefits for all stakeholders.

As a principal, I was in every classroom at least once a day. My visits were not to evaluate teachers but, on the contrary, were to motivate and assist teachers in their work. I would often become an active participant in the lesson. At times, I would help teach the lesson and other times I would assist students who were in need of extra help. Through this daily positive interaction with teachers and students, a relationship of trust and teamwork is built. Once this relationship of trust is built, the path to achieving the goal of all students being successful becomes clearer.

As administrators, principals are knowledgeable about what is going on and not going on in classrooms. Therefore, we are able to help orchestrate a plan based on observation, combined with other data gathered to help students and teachers move to the next level.

As an administrator, we are pulled in thousands of directions; therefore, we must put into our daily schedule time for classroom visits. Make sure that your secretary and others know that this is sacred time. Meetings and other issues will need to be worked around these times. When your teachers and community see that being an active part of classroom instruction is your first priority, they will support your schedule and work with you to arrange meetings around your classroom time.

ZILKER IS A GREAT PLACE FOR KIDS!

Ramona S. Trevino
Austin, Texas

At Zilker Elementary School, we worked to establish an environment for creative and active school community participation with both purpose and focus. Zilker's motto is "Zilker is a great place for kids!" The truth is that it is a great place for all who enter its doors. I am often reminded how warm and friendly Zilker feels. It was a prime objective of mine to lead in creating a climate of respect and support, and this has happened, as we have many new, fun, and entertaining ways to build parental and community support.

We established Casa Zilker, our parenting center and clothes closet, and provided ESL classes, toddler story time, and the Baby Panther infant program. Events have been created to promote and respect our community. They include La Posadas, Diez y Seis, and Cinco de Mayo potluck dinners and concerts, Sixth Grade Banquet, Curriculum Night, Texas Assessment of Academic Skills (TAAS) information night, Girls' Brown Bag Luncheons, Zilker Fun Run, Coffee House Talent Show, Principal's Coffees, Arts in Education Benefit Concert, and Sock Hop.

A school brochure was created and a school marquee built to promote Zilker. Our parents built a breathtaking outdoor learning center in which our community gathers for many of these events. After a year of implementing a schoolwide unit of study on the history of Zilker, the spirit of our school was embraced and celebrated on a grand scale. We often say that our goal is not just about fundraising, but mostly "funraising." Embracing the many talents of our parents and bringing all factions of our community together in a common spirit of celebration and support has produced an extended nested learning community.

Tradition and Progress Are Key

Kathleen Genovese Haworth
North Hollywood, California

Laurel Hall School is in its 56th year of serving the San Fernando Valley/North Hollywood area, which is a suburb of the city of Los Angeles. The school is a member of the Evangelical Lutheran Education Association, which is a division or ministry of the Evangelical Lutheran Church of America. We have three classes of each grade level. However, in the last few years, our largest student growth spurt has been in the middle school, Grades 6 through 8. I have been a school principal for 11 years, the last 7 with Laurel Hall.

Tradition and progress are the keys to our school's success. We have a strong faculty who take a personal interest in the students. We strive to embrace a holistic approach to education, recognizing that academics and test scores, while important, are only a portion of the educational accountability we need to consider. We make every effort to provide a balance of educational opportunities that encompass the emotional, social, and spiritual development of all children. Our faculty is innovative and works as a team to provide nurturing role models in our community. At Laurel Hall, we offer the students a wide variety of programs in athletics, the arts, and technology that complement our strong academic program. Through exposure to these various programs, we take pride in watching our students develop skills and interests and discover their individual talents. We welcome input from parents, students, and faculty to introduce new programs on a regular basis.

As a school, we are very proud of the process that we have developed in resolving conflicts. We articulate the philosophy that student success is always at the forefront in each situation. We devote a great deal of time gathering facts when there is a problem involving students and families. While our policies guide each situation, we recognize that each child and issue is individual and that final decisions need to reflect a life-learning lesson that will assist the student in making positive future choices. Depending on the complexity of the situation, we work as a team and make sure that all voices are heard. As a school in a church-based setting, we can also build grace into the overall interpretation of otherwise black-and-white school policies.

Los Angeles, like many cities, is a big area. Families are looking for a sense of community. Laurel Hall offers ample opportunities throughout the school year for families to be involved in the lives of their children. We want our families to be involved with both classroom activities and schoolwide events. Each year, we invite parents to serve on committees to plan Homecoming, the Harvest Festival, Grandparents' Day, and the Spring Fair. Other classroom events include activities such as the third grade Japanese tea ceremony, the sixth grade science demonstration, mock trial, and all-school art show and instrumental programs. Equally important as the sense of community is safety. Laurel Hall opens its doors every day at 6:45 a.m. and remains open until 6:00 p.m. Families feel assured in leaving their children, some for over 11 hours each day, that our staff is responsive and sensitive to individual and campuswide emergencies.

Snapshots

Muffins for Mom and Donuts for Dad

Cindy Gipson
Raymond, Mississippi

In an effort to increase the number of parents that come to school during the school day to see their children actively engaged in school activities, we created two special days. Moms come one day for muffins and dads come on another day for donuts. We work closely with the sheriff's department and community organizations to provide substitute dads and moms for children from single-parent families. Moms and dads enjoy having muffins and donuts with their children. Then they are escorted to the computer lab, where students demonstrate their knowledge of one computer lesson with their parents' assistance. What a beautiful sight to see children and parents enjoying time together in learning!

Working Side by Side

Marla W. McGhee
Austin, Texas

We rolled up our shirt sleeves and worked side by side. I never asked teachers to do something I was not willing to do. I attended staff development alongside staff, audited reading recovery training, became a trainer for the New Jersey Writing Project in Texas, went to Marilyn Burns mathematics training sessions, and many other things.

Positive School Climate

Sharon Roemer
Arroyo Grande, California

Ocean View Elementary School's Star Student program is a schoolwide systematic approach for building a positive school climate around self-esteem, social skills, and personal responsibility. It is a program that gives children the tools for developing skills in ethical decision making. Each morning I give the students a one-minute motivational message based on a different theme each month such as respect, responsibility, or trustworthiness. One class from every two grade levels presents a short skit along with a poster describing the theme for that month. The skits are performed in the cafeteria during lunch periods. In addition, teachers teach short lessons in class on each theme. Then during the month, teachers and other staff give tickets to those students practicing good decision-making skills. The tickets are collected in jars located in the school cafeteria. At the end of the month, tickets are pulled to select students who receive prizes.

Reading Buddies

Robert W. Fowls
Bend, Oregon

At the beginning of each year, we match up our younger students with a "buddy" from an upper grade. We facilitate times for these buddies to get together, such as reading times, computer lab experiences, going to chapel services together, and even going on field trips together as classes with their buddies. It develops relationships that directly benefit the entire climate of our school, as well as the individual buddies.

Playing Classical Music

Scott Hollinger
McAllen, Texas

We play classical music outdoors and in the hallways 24-7-365. We connected a 200-CD player to our school's intercom system. We turn on the speakers in the halls and the exterior horns. When parents and visitors arrive at our school, they hear classical music playing as soon as they park their cars. The music sets a tone around the building that says, "This is a smart place."

Shaking Hands

Scott Hollinger
McAllen, Texas

Everyone in our school shakes hands. We actually teach our students how to do it (eye contact, lean in, smile, "web-to-web" grip: firm but not crushing). Then, as students arrive at school and enter the gym, they shake hands with a staff member at the door. During morning assembly, they shake hands with three other people. After they leave the gym, every child in the school shakes hands with his or her teacher before entering the classroom. Sometimes a helper stands with the teacher at the classroom door. Every child in my school gets at least five appropriate touches before classes begin!

SHAPING CAMPUS CULTURE REFLECTION

1. How would I characterize the culture on our school campus?
2. What do I do well on our campus to shape and maintain a positive campus culture?
3. What do I need to do to improve our campus culture?
4. What groups do I communicate with for greater community involvement in shaping and maintaining our campus culture?
5. Which ideas in this chapter do I especially like?
6. How can we implement these ideas in our school?
7. How might they need to be revised to be most effective at our school?

ADDITIONAL RESOURCES

Capturing Kids' Hearts
http://www.leadershipsolutions.com/educ_ckh.html

Conflict Resolution
http://www.csmp.org

Early Literacy Program
http://www.literacy.uconn.edu/earlit.htm
http://www.yale.edu/21c/resourcebank.html

Four-Block Reading
http://www.blocks4reading.com

Peace Pledge
http://www.main.nc.us/peacelinks/index.html

Project Reconnect
http://www.houstonisd.org

Reading Recovery
http://www.readingrecovery.com

Texas Mentor School Network
http://www.tea.state.tx.us/taa/com010402.html

REFERENCES

Boyer, E. (1995). *The basic school*. Princeton, NJ: Carnegie Foundation for the Advancement of Teaching.

Brewer, J. (1998). *Introduction to early childhood education* (3rd ed.). Boston: Allyn & Bacon.

Calkin, L. (1994). *The art of teaching writing* (2nd ed.). Portsmouth, NH: Heinemann.

Collaborating and Communicating

To perform like a team, act like a team—together.

—Roland S. Barth

Roland S. Barth (2003), in his book *Lessons Learned*, challenges principals to collaborate through shared leadership. This allows leaders to "become not 'heroes' but 'hero makers'" (p. 63). Of course, a key ingredient in successful collaboration is good communication. When principals effectively communicate the vision of the school, a greater commitment to students is nurtured at all levels of the school community.

Our award-winning principals emphasized that as they seek to build effective school experiences for children, they draw on the collective talents of the learning community through collaboration and communication. Exerta T. Mackie describes the team approach that has helped her become an award-winning principal. John Ciesluk shares how to build a school climate, and Ann Porter tells how communication helped her establish an important connection with staff members at a new school after her school was destroyed by a devastating flood. Sharon L. Vestermark illustrates how school visitation days both involve parents and result in improved instruction. Other principals describe what they are doing to bring the professional community and the family into the school through parent and community involvement programs, writing notes, providing programs that honor American heroes, helping students transition smoothly into middle school, and involving young children in community service.

THE TEAM APPROACH

Exerta T. Mackie
Houston, Texas

My leadership style has always been entrenched in a team approach; therefore, I steadfastly believe that "it takes a village to raise the child." It is to this perception that I attribute my success. Upon my arrival at Kashmere Gardens Elementary School, the faculty and I began by assessing the school's mission statement: To "interlace a concentrated curriculum with a unified effort of teachers, parents, and community to provide an instructional program that prepares students to excel as contributors to a global society." The administration, faculty, and support staff provide a variety of services to meet the needs of our varied student population while preparing them for academic challenges of the future.

The staff realizes that the success of students is dependent upon the integration of curriculum objectives, relentless instruction, and accurate assessment. Our instruction is tailored to provide high expectations intertwined with academic excellence. To ensure this, we provide departmentalized instruction, flexible grouping, teacher looping, and tutorials (seventh-hour, afterschool, Saturday). Our assessment process is ongoing in order to monitor student progress and adjust instruction.

To address the needs of the whole child, a variety of extracurricular activities are available for our students. The school service activities include, but are not limited to, Student Council, Announcers' Guild, and Health Club. The Fine Arts Department offers chorus, keyboard, dance, and drama, while the Library Club, Science Club, and Computer Club are academically based. Thus, we provide opportunities to identify and develop the individual talents and interests of every student.

Staff members are required to attend periodic staff development opportunities from various venues, including our own weekly staff development. These sessions include grade-level collaboration, vertical alignment of curriculum, department teaming, and teacher training. Under my leadership, utilization of campus-based expertise, as well as outside consultants, is emphasized.

Project Reconnect, designed to reconnect the community with the schools, provides a Parent Center coordinated by a parent educator. Our parent educator is available daily to encourage parent and community participation in school activities and to provide educational opportunities, such as ESL, GED preparation, computer literacy, and self-improvement classes. Parents who are engaged in school and community activities model a high standard of success for their children, thus ensuring the children an equal start educationally.

To this village (administrator, teachers and staff, parents, and community) I attribute Kashmere Gardens's success!

Establishing Climate Through Communicating

John Ciesluk
Longmeadow, Massachusetts

Principals demonstrate exceptional interpersonal skills. They communicate with others in an effective and open manner. At Wolf Swamp Road Elementary School, everyone's ideas are considered in support of the learning community. As principal, I utilize the school's organizational structure and daily routines to seek input from teachers, parents, and students alike. Important decisions, changes in routines, or upcoming events are communicated through a variety of meetings and publications. The school publishes a monthly newsletter called *The Scribbler,* which includes articles from all aspects of the school community. In addition, the school has a page on the district's Web site that the school's Web master manages.

My door is always open. Parents, teachers, and students stop by to ask a question, express a concern, or suggest an improvement in daily routines. I greet all students by name every day as they arrive on the school grounds and wave them good-bye at the end of the day. The school is a neighborhood school that does not utilize buses. We call this the "live line," and it provides an important way to touch base with parents on a daily basis.

Parents have a strong voice at Wolf Swamp Road School. I meet with the PTO co-presidents almost daily and the executive board weekly. This important link to the community provides effective two-way communication. Rarely do sleeping giants emerge and surprise parents, teachers, or the administration.

When students misbehave, parents are expected to play a role in making corrective action. It is important that students know they can make mistakes, but they are expected to know what they need to do to improve their behavior.

Celebrations and special events contribute to the inviting climate that exists at the school. The PTO and School Spirit Committee plan assemblies, luncheons and coffees, picnics, and such special events as Hockey Night, roller skating parties, and field days. A day does not go by without someone extolling the warm, caring atmosphere that exists at our school. Without a doubt, the most critical element in creating this climate is the warm welcome that everyone receives from the office staff as they enter the building.

Morning Assembly Fosters a Communicative School Culture

Scott Hollinger
McAllen, Texas

We are a large elementary school with over 800 students. Although our community culture is strong, it's easy for students and staff on one side of the school to begin to feel disconnected from the students and staff on the other side of the school. Our morning assembly is a time every day that the whole school comes together to celebrate our unity.

Each school day morning, all teachers and students report to the gym before classes begin. When the bell rings, an upbeat "gathering" song, played via the public address system, signals students to sit cross-legged on the floor by class. The gathering song is followed immediately by the national anthem, student-led pledges to the American and Texas flags, and a moment of silence. The remainder of the assembly includes announcements for students and teachers, recognition of classes that had perfect attendance the previous day, recognition of birthdays with everyone singing "Happy Birthday," student-read essays, and discussion of social skills. Each assembly closes with a song that the whole school sings. Classes exit the gym to more upbeat music. The assembly takes 10 to 15 minutes.

Teachers report that morning assembly is a community-building way to start the school day. At least 30 parents attend morning assembly every morning. Teachers, students, and staff use morning assembly as a vehicle for communicating with the entire school. For example, during Book Fair week, the librarian selected one student each day to read an essay about books and reading. The fourth grade "advertises" their fundraiser so they can earn the money to take a field trip to San Antonio to visit the Alamo at the end of the year.

You don't need a gym or a large auditorium to make morning assembly work for you. We started outdoors, lining up by classes on the blacktop, and playing our music on a large sound system that we mounted on a rolling cart.

Bloom Where You Are Planted

Ann Porter
Grand Forks, North Dakota

When my school closed after our community experienced a devastating flood in 1997, I was assigned to another neighborhood school. In order to get to know a new staff, I wrote a letter and included a self-addressed, stamped envelope. I asked staff to respond to three questions to help me understand this new place where I would find myself planted. The questions were the following:

1. What do you want me to know about you?

2. What do you want me to know about Lewis & Clark School?

3. What do you want Lewis & Clark School to be?

The answers to these questions gave me a good idea of the first place I would concentrate my time and energies. The staff over and over again wrote about the need for respect in the school. So I began where I had some ideas and thought I could make a difference. The school had a new lunchroom after the flood, so new rules and procedures and a new attitude were in order.

Working with lunchroom staff, I described my vision for the lunchroom:

1. We would promote a family atmosphere. Each session would have multiple age groups. Through the years, I have found that having children of different ages

together eliminates a number of behavior issues. One reason is that the youngest have never experienced this setting and are so excited about being there that they require a great deal of our supervisors' time and energy to teach, practice, and reteach the lunchroom expectations. If they were all in the same session, the helpers would be spread much too thin. In addition, the older students can be big brothers and sisters for the younger students by being good examples and helpers. This leadership role for the older students reduces the number of behavior problems they are often responsible for.

2. Students had called supervisors by their first names. To send the message that these adults had authority to implement the rules and procedures, supervisors were to be addressed as Mrs., Ms., or Mr. Name tags were ordered for all staff members, including lunchroom supervisors, identifying their role in our school. This small thing sent the message that all staff adults had just as important a role in creating a respectful school climate as the faculty.

3. Previously, students would pick up their food trays, sit down to eat, and leave for recess as soon as possible. Again, to promote a family atmosphere, students picked up their food trays, sat down to eat, then were expected to remain seated until it was time for the class to be excused. This promoted informal conversation among the students and staff. Many of our students do not have a regular sit-down meal with their families. As I interacted with students, I learned that some did not even have a kitchen table in their house or apartment. Eating on the run might be acceptable in our students' homes, but it would not be at our school.

The lunchroom team met monthly to identify what was going well and what needed improvement. That first year was exceptionally challenging. The older students were rebellious as the boundaries for lunchroom behavior were reined in. It became my job to role-model appropriate interactions with students, to guide and encourage lunchroom workers to persevere, and to provide positive feedback.

Lunchroom staff continue to meet regularly to support one another, to update rules and procedures, and to share ideas. Some of the changes we have made include the following:

1. Supervisors began wearing aprons with large pockets in which they carried extra napkins and silverware. I also wore an apron when I was in the lunchroom to send the message that *the principal is on your team.*

2. Lunchroom staff sponsored two dress-up days (Christmas and Valentine's Day) to promote good manners. Students were asked to wear their best dress-up clothes. The staff dressed up too, and our custodian even wore a waiter's tux one year. Tables were set with centerpieces and favors. We had fun while teaching that manners help us all to get along.

3. A number of our staff were trained in teaching and parenting with Teaching With Love and Logic and provided staff with minilessons at staff meetings. We wanted our support staff to be on board with teachers. So the counselor met with the lunchroom staff weekly at the beginning of the year to teach the strategies and language of Teaching With Love and Logic. Each received a book they could take home, read, and keep for reference. Out of these meetings came several ideas. One was to use a "yakker tracker" to monitor the noise level. This device flashes green when the noise level is appropriate, yellow when it is getting louder, and makes a screeching noise when the room is too loud. This allows students to self-monitor and be responsible for the noise level in the lunchroom. It also permits supervisors to serve students until the yakker tracker goes off. It was one step above a green, yellow, and red card system we had used the previous year.

Working and teaching in the lunchroom remains a challenge, but our staff have been willing to take it on enthusiastically. Last year the fifth graders had been kindergartners when I arrived at Lewis & Clark. We were all proud of the lifelong learners and responsible citizens they had become. It takes time and patience to see the results of our work. When you see the difference it can make, it is motivating to continue the important job we have chosen.

Promote Community Relations

Gina Segobiano
Belleville, Illinois

The superintendent and principal are the educational leaders in the school district. The community relies upon their leadership to provide an excellent education for the students attending the school. It is imperative to communicate pertinent and positive accomplishments about your school to the stakeholders in the district in order to gain support and a sense of school pride in the community. More and more, the job of the educational leader is to not only be the instructional leader for your faculty and students but to also develop positive public relations among the parents and community in order to gain continual support and school pride.

Property values are directly linked to the success of the school district within the community. Community members must be assured that the school district is providing all students with an exceptional education and high levels of achievement. Bottom line—good schools attract home buyers. Administrators have the responsibility to communicate the success of the school district among all residents living within the district.

There are several steps administrators can take to gain support and to build relations with all stakeholders. The first and foremost is to introduce yourself and let yourself be known to the community. When someone asks who is the principal at this school or who is the superintendent at that school, parents and community members should be quick to respond. If the residents do not know the answer to that question, the principal and superintendent have a lot of work ahead. Community members should know by name the educational leader in their community. Here are just a few steps that administrators can take to build positive home-school relationships and to promote your school within the community:

Be Visible

- In the morning, stand in front of school and welcome parents and students to school!
- Circulate at dismissal and initiate conversations with a variety of parents. Be sure to introduce yourself to all parents. Don't talk to the same parent every morning or every day after school. Mingle!
- Make a point to attend sporting events as much as possible, particularly when you are not "assigned" to supervise. That way, you can sit with the parents and/or converse freely with attendees.
- No matter what, a good administrator knows every student's name. Address the students by name each morning. Parents will be shocked that you personally know the students.
- Attend all PTO events and circulate! Don't just sit, listen, and leave. Talk to the parents and students. Ask how they are doing. Get to know the families in your district by name.

Community Involvement

- Get to know your community. Drive through the neighborhoods to fully understand the socioeconomic breakdown of your students' environments.
- Become a member of a local organization such as the chamber of commerce, Optimist Club, or Rotary Club.

Make sure your students participate in activities to
ensure that your school's name and students' names are
printed in the program.

- Attend community events: fall festivals, picnics, celebrations. Wear a school sweatshirt when taking a walk
in the neighborhood.
- Go to the high school's events. Check on your alumni
and speak to your "past" parents.
- Invite leaders from your neighborhood associations (if
you have them) to a breakfast at your school to introduce yourself and to provide school information.
- Invite key business leaders in your community to
school to discuss possible school-business partnerships.

Publications

- Publish a monthly newsletter that includes a message
from the principal. Also, be sure to include student
accomplishments with digital pictures. Parents love to
see pictures of students learning.
- Make sure your school has a brochure to distribute to
new families and real estate agents.
- More and more people check the Web. The school's Web
site should be up to date and thorough, including a lot
of information that would be meaningful to potential
new homeowners. The Web site should portray a welcoming and nurturing climate.
- Send press releases to your local newspaper on a regular basis. Highlight PTO events, classroom activities,
assemblies, student accomplishments, and more. Let
the newspaper know what your students are doing for
the various holidays.

Other

- Conduct monthly PTO events that focus on the
students. Art Fair, Young Author Night, Open House,
Science Fair, Math Night, and more bring tons of
parents into your building. Make sure your building

celebrates learning by having the halls decorated with student work.

- Make sure school T-shirts and sweatshirts are available for students to purchase and wear. In turn, the students will wear the school T-shirts and sweatshirts around the neighborhood and community at large. Have Spirit Days or School Color Days to promote school pride.
- Always have an open door and be available for parents who need a question answered.
- Remember, a positive attitude and a friendly smile go a long way!

COMMUNITY AND PARENT INVOLVEMENT

Lori Musser
Joplin, Missouri

Community involvement is strong at Columbia Elementary School. Our school has specific business partners in the community (Southwest Missouri Bank and Joplin Family YMCA) with whom we work closely to provide opportunities and resources for our students to help support our curriculum and instruction. Other area businesses donate meal certificates to students who make good grades and have good school attendance. Area businesses such as Papa Johns and Keeley's Skating Rink designate some nights as Columbia Night, where Columbia is the beneficiary of a percentage of proceeds from sales for that night. Pizza Hut provides free pizza certificates to students, based on their reading achievements. These interactions aid in increasing students' self-esteem and contribute to our positive atmosphere.

Guest speakers from our community are also incorporated to support our curriculum. "Indian Joe" visits Columbia to speak to students about Native American heritage and culture. The local firefighters and police officers provide safety programs for our students. Local veterans and active military personnel also provide insight into civic duty, world relations, and government. The local sheltered workshop provides an insightful and positive presentation to our students about people with disabilities and incorporates the use of puppets and music into their presentation.

Our community businesses realize the importance of high academic achievement and quality students within our community and have put forth the effort to encourage our students and families to succeed. Academic All-Stars is a program that was developed as a collaborative effort between local CEOs, parents, and school personnel. Students who score "proficient" or "advanced" on the state-mandated Missouri Assessment Program (MAP) test are recognized, and a ceremony is held in their honor. Students receive a certificate, T-shirt, and several prizes from area businesses.

Columbia has several programs that involve families in their children's education because parents are the central contributors to their students' education and achievement. Columbia supports and enhances the parenting role with programs through the incorporation of parent volunteers and tutors. These programs invite family members into the classroom to be involved in the learning process and to share. Family Literacy Night also takes place two times throughout the year. Students and their parents are invited to come to school and attend various literacy activities.

Student planners are utilized in Grades 3 to 5 to enhance communication with parents. The students take their planners home every day for parents to review and sign. Assignments, tests, and important communications are recorded in the planners.

Terrific Tuesdays is another special communication program. Every Tuesday, classroom teachers select a few students in their room and contact those students' parents with something positive. Three newsletters are sent home each month. Our *Home and School Connection* newsletter and the *Early Literacy News* provide applicable activities and ideas for parents in helping their children be successful. The PTO newsletter focuses on school events and occurrences in an effort to keep parents informed.

Thursday Folders are used in the fourth grade to enhance communication and involve families in their children's education. Each Thursday students take home a folder with their completed and graded work for the week inside. Parents sign the folder, write comments, and return it to school the next morning. Our primary and special education teachers send home daily reading logs for parents to provide and document reading time at home. Parent-teacher conferences, where parents meet with their children's teachers to discuss and plan for their children's achievement and success in school, also involve parents in their students' education. Flexible scheduling takes place for these conferences so that they are convenient for the parents. Parents are encouraged to get involved in PTO, become parent volunteers or room mothers, and attend school board meetings so they can become more involved in decisions and communications.

BRINGING PROFESSIONALS INTO THE SCHOOL COMMUNITY

Rod Smith
Lenexa, Kansas

Our school has a program called Authors & Illustrators. The purpose of the program is to bring professionals into the school from the local community and teach the students the *value* of writing and illustration in their professional career. We have had writers from the *Kansas City Star* newspaper, creators of Hallmark Cards, local engineers and architects, TV ad writers from Godfather's Pizza, and artists from the local art gallery and private practice visit our school to share with the students.

The writing activities tie in closely with our *school improvement* goal for writing. It gives students opportunities to see that the writing they do and the model (Six Traits of Writing) they use to become proficient writers connect with being a *great* writer some day.

We complete the morning sessions with a luncheon in the school library provided by the PTA. The luncheon is our way to thank our guests. Part of the luncheon is an opportunity for each guest speaker to tell the others the topic they presented and what the children learned. The students, teachers, and parents report this as a *true* highlight each year.

CONSTANT COMMUNICATION

Dawn Smith
Warm Springs, Oregon

Constantly keeping the school community informed and updated is one of the most important tasks of the building leader (individual or shared leadership model). The more people within the school community (staff, parents, community members, etc.) who understand the school vision, goals, instructional and assessment programs, data, successes, and challenges, the less anyone is taken by surprise when program changes and adjustments are needed. Genuine collaboration and communication within the school community builds trust, the foundation for effective schooling.

Just last year, we added a communication tool based on parent responses to a survey asking for more information on *what* was being taught in the classroom. Teachers, while completing weekly lesson plans, sketch out the coming week plans for the core academic subjects and send them home with students each Monday. This keeps parents informed of what is coming up academically and what their children will miss if they are absent from school. Having these plans has led parents to begin to ask for more "how information"—how are the concepts and skills being taught in the classroom so that they can get a better feel for helping their children at home. The simple one-page sketch of the coming week has now become a multipage packet of information that goes home to parents and has opened the door for more in-depth, informal parent-teacher conferencing. It's been great!

A word of caution though: Do not assume that the parents of your children use print as their primary access to information. Many families across many different ethnic and socioeconomic lines do not. For many parents, frequent opportunities to visit the school informally and oral information given out at gatherings and over the radio are just as helpful and sometimes more helpful.

Parent Volunteers and the Breakfast Book Club

Carol Loflin
San Ramon, California

One program we have developed is our Breakfast Book Club. Over one-third of our 450 students participate. The entire program is run by parent volunteers. Once a month, students who have signed up for the club meet in our multiuse room 45 minutes before school starts. A committee of parents provides breakfast (donuts and donut holes, fruit, hot chocolate, orange juice). While the students eat breakfast, an adult reads a story to the group. It is usually a short story with a special message, possibly coinciding with a life skill on which the school is focusing.

During the previous Breakfast Book Club meeting, all students at each grade level are given a copy of a particular book that they are to read for the next meeting. With the help of the classroom teachers, grade-appropriate, high-interest books are selected for each grade level. After breakfast, students break into grade-level groups and go into an assigned classroom. A team of parent volunteers then leads a discussion about the book the students have read that month. Each month our parents lead meaningful discussions about books and then the students get a copy of a new book that they will read for the next month's meeting.

At the last meeting of the year, students bring books for a book exchange so that they can select some new books for the summer. This is a wonderful way to continue a focus on literacy, provide an opportunity for parents to be involved, and make reading fun!

SCHOOL VISITATION DAYS FOR PARENTAL INVOLVEMENT AND IMPROVED INSTRUCTION

Sharon L. Vestermark
Laguna Hills, California

One of the challenges in including parents in school leadership is striking a comfortable balance between the decisions parents are asked to make and their knowledge of the total school program. Parents need to feel assured that their input is informed and valued and that they are not being asked to rubber-stamp staff wishes. To find this balance, several years ago when I was principal at an elementary school with a large second language and special education population and many new teachers, the staff and I decided to offer a school visitation day. I believed that many of the newer teachers and those who worked primarily with second language or special education students were not well known by the parent community and therefore were not receiving the respect or recognition they deserved. In addition, the parent leadership was being asked to make many decisions but often had little information on which to base their actions.

Through our School Site Council (SSC), a parent and staff steering committee, a school visitation day was planned. The

SSC chose the focus for the visit; for example, during a math adoption year, they chose to observe math lessons. The following year we analyzed differentiated instruction and meeting the needs of all learners. I recruited several of the newer, special education, and second language teachers to volunteer their classrooms as visitation sites and prepared them for what the parents would be observing. In addition to the SSC, the PTA executive board was invited to participate. Staff members who served on the SSC were given a release day so that they too could be involved.

The morning began with an overview of the area of focus. Participants identified questions they had, and staff members shared two to three instructional techniques and strategies the group could expect to see. Visitors received a feedback sheet and then visited two classrooms at different grade levels for about 30 minutes each. Following the classroom visits, the observers reconvened and debriefed, sharing what they had observed.

The visitation day gave me an opportunity to educate parents about curricular issues and instructional strategies. It turned into a valuable public relations tool. The process was helpful also, as more teachers were able to be in the spotlight and parents were able to know staff members with whom they might otherwise not become acquainted. Even parents who regularly volunteered in their students' classrooms learned the nuances of some instructional techniques and developed a greater appreciation for the art of teaching. An added, and unanticipated, benefit was that the teachers who served on SSC were able to observe colleagues whom they never saw in the teaching role. These teachers received positive feedback and accolades and often were asked to share one of the strategies they had demonstrated. Evaluations of the day were consistently positive, and each year more teachers offered their classrooms as observation sites.

COMMUNITY SERVICE

Lori Musser
Joplin, Missouri

Community service is an ever-growing and increasingly important goal at Columbia Elementary School. Each grade level adopts a community service agency. This year we worked with local agencies such as the Ronald McDonald House, Lafayette House (a shelter for parents and children who are victims of domestic violence), Soul's Harbor (a homeless shelter), and the local Humane Society. During the holiday season, our students collect nonperishable food items, hats, gloves, scarves, and toys for area agencies such as the Salvation Army and Soul's Harbor. Columbia students also supported six of our own needy families by providing food baskets during the holidays.

Students also go Christmas caroling at local senior citizen homes and provide them and other area senior citizens with homemade cards at Christmas and on Valentine's Day. A veterans' lunch was provided for local veterans on Veteran's Day. Students collected change after the September 11 tragedies and donated approximately $600 to that fund. Our kindergarten students adopted our area Humane Society and donated over 100 bags of dog and cat food. Our student council spends the proceeds from the school store to meet school needs.

Our PTO and business partners worked very closely with our school to improve the playground and obtained a grant to purchase new equipment. This not only benefited Columbia students but also the surrounding neighborhood community by providing a safe, enjoyable place for the children to play. Columbia faculty and staff members donate school supplies to have on hand for current or new students who are unable to afford them.

Columbia students also participate in several community-sponsored contests such as the Martin Luther King Poster Contest, the Chamber of Commerce Community Pride Starts Inside Essay Contest, and the Children's Haven Logo Contest.

Our teachers and staff are themselves involved in volunteering in our community in a variety of ways in order to build a stronger relationship between school and community and to perform their own civic duties. Some area organizations that benefit from our faculty and staff participation include area churches, charitable organizations, Boys and Girls Clubs, youth sports programs, and 4-H. We also recycle paper, cardboard, telephone books, and aluminum cans in an effort to improve our community environment.

SNAPSHOTS

Involved Parents Help the Budget

John Ciesluk
Longmeadow, Massachusetts

At Wolf Swamp Road Elementary School, the principal manages several budget accounts to fund professional development activities, and the PTO plays a key role in supplementing those funds. Annually, the PTO supports approximately 20 registrations for workshops and 5 to 10 teacher summer institutes. In addition, teachers are encouraged to apply for the Longmeadow Educational Enrichment Fund (LEEF) grants. Wolf Swamp teachers received 3 of the 17 district LEEF grants this past fall.

Parents fill key roles as volunteers in the school. They serve as computer workstation helpers, math pretest and posttest correctors, and kindergarten helpers. One of the most sophisticated programs that parents coordinate is a fourth grade parent volunteer writing program, which involves 12 parents on a weekly basis. Parents also coordinate and run a program called Family Math Nights. Parents see all and do all at Wolf Swamp Road School.

Parent Center

Scott Hollinger
McAllen, Texas

Our district and our school are hurting for space, so it's a really big deal that we have reserved an entire classroom at our school for parents. Before we had our Parent Center, we had about two parent volunteers at a time—largely because the volunteers didn't have a place to call their own. Now we often have as many as 15 volunteers at a time. The Parent Center includes work tables, a living room area, a classroom area, and a kitchen with refrigerator, sink, microwave, coffee maker, and various electric cookers. Parents often gather here just to chat but soon end up laminating, cutting, and sorting. It was a direct result of our Parent Center that we finally succeeded in getting parents and teachers to work together in the classroom!

Write Three Notes a Day

Paul Young
Lancaster, Ohio

As a beginning principal, I tried to absorb every bit of advice I could. While attending a workshop just weeks before beginning my first principalship, I heard this tip from a veteran Columbus (Ohio) public school principal. Unfortunately, I've forgotten her name. But the advice I gleaned from her has provided favorable returns on my investment of time and energy for nearly 20 years.

Write three notes daily. Make sure they are handwritten on nice stationery. Focus on identifying the special things that people do to help make the school run smoothly. Write notes to teachers, students, parents, volunteers, community members—anyone who connects with your school and your job and makes it a special place.

Writing personal notes allows you to reinforce your expectations and to commend positive behavior and job performance in a quiet, personal manner. Clip articles from the newspaper and include copies with your handwritten note. People will love the attention and recognition.

Encourage your teachers to do the same. I've visited many students' homes during my tenure as a principal and more often than not found notes proudly displayed on refrigerators and other visible locations. They become treasured items.

Think of the positives you will generate! Three a day adds up over time. It sets a tone. You won't regret the effort.

Weekly Teacher Newsletter

Scott Hollinger
McAllen, Texas

Each week, I produce a professional-looking two-page newsletter for teachers. During the week, I jot down every topic that at one time might have triggered a memo or an e-mail. Then, on Friday, I write all those topics as articles in the newsletter. The weekly newsletter also includes reminders of next week's duty assignments, book study groups, other important dates and deadlines, and staff birthdays. The newsletter includes staff development notices, kudos for staff, personal news (when appropriate), and a humor piece. To get a professional look, I use 20-pound bond paper, printed at a local print shop with my school's logo, and the newsletter's masthead in color. Then (just like a church bulletin) I run the preprinted shells through our school's photocopier to produce the newsletter.

Martin Luther King Jr. Program

Rod Smith
Lenexa, Kansas

This program is the only existing program of its kind in our *entire* school district. We want children to learn about the life, accomplishments, and significance of Martin Luther King Jr. The program originated when the teachers in the fifth grade decided the students should find a way to honor Dr. King besides the holiday away from school.

This program aligns with district curriculum. It is cross-curricular. It allows teachers to teach diversity through music, social studies, and reading. Students learn so much from this program through the research, oral presentations, and drama. As a result of this program, students have gained a greater appreciation for the life of Dr. King.

This program has been performed at the local library the Sunday before the Martin Luther King Jr. holiday. The all-school program is done on a Friday. The dramatic presentation is such a great way to teach students about diversity. By having it at the local library, the students and their teacher give back to the community while teaching them about the impact Dr. King had on society.

Volunteers in Reading

Sharon Roemer
Arroyo Grande, California

Ocean View Elementary School is fortunate to have many active parent and community volunteers who are trained in tutoring techniques in the reading process by credentialed teachers. Volunteers are trained in reading together strategies, decoding strategies that children use, conversations about reading, and making a read-write connection. The tutors work one-on-one with individual students for 30 minutes twice a week. Parents of selected students are asked for permission for their child to participate in this program. Our young readers benefit from this individual attention and extra time that supports their emerging reading skills.

Family Reading Night

Rod Smith
Lenexa, Kansas

We want children at our school to *learn* to read and *love* to read. Each year during Kansas READ Week we schedule Family Reading Night. The activities and presentations are done *completely* by our teachers. The sessions are organized for the parents to attend with their children. We structure them so that primary and intermediate students can access the sessions that fit their age. Some of the session's titles are Who Wants to be a Reading Millionaire, ABC-Chicka-a-Chicka Boom Boom, Exercise Your Right to Read, and the Trial of Hansel and Gretel. These sessions integrate drama, science, art, storytelling, and a host of other curricular ideas into the presentations. Each year the parents and students enjoy a menu of approximately 30 sessions.

This program has been a *huge* success at our school. Around 400 to 500 parents and students attend. The message that "reading is important" gets promoted over and over. The evening provides an opportunity to experience different ways to enrich literature. The activities are both fun and meaningful.

Transition to Middle School

Lori Musser
Joplin, Missouri

Special care is taken at Columbia Elementary School to help our fifth graders easily transition to middle school. Toward the end of the fifth grade year, the counselors and administrators from the middle school visit Columbia to enroll our students and address their questions and concerns. A special day is scheduled for our fifth grade students to visit the middle school and shadow a sixth grader throughout the whole day. This helps our students to see what a day is like at middle school and exposes them to the procedures and routines. A meeting also takes place between Columbia personnel and special education personnel from the middle school to individually plan for the transitions of our students with special needs.

COLLABORATING AND COMMUNICATING REFLECTION

1. In what ways do I encourage collaboration at our school?
2. In what ways can I improve collaborative efforts at our school?
3. How do I communicate most effectively with the school community?
4. In what ways can I communicate better with the school community?
5. Which ideas in this chapter do I especially like?
6. How can we implement these ideas in our school?
7. How might they need to be revised to be successful?

ADDITIONAL RESOURCES

Lafayette House
http://mocasa.missouri.org/dvshltr.htm

Ronald McDonald House
http://www.rmhc.org

Salvation Army
http://www.salvationarmyusa.org

Teaching with Love and Logic
http://www.loveandlogic.com

REFERENCE

Barth, R. (2003). *Lessons learned*. Thousand Oaks, CA: Corwin.

Effective
Instructional
Programs

Learning is not attained by chance. It must be sought for with ardor and attended to with diligence.

—Abigail Adams

Recognizing the powerful effect on student learning that happens in the classroom, a major role of the principal is to be the instructional leader on the school campus. For this reason, Anita and Wayne Hoy (2003), in *Instructional Leadership: A Learning-Centered Guide,* challenge principals to improve instruction by "providing a school culture and climate where change is linked to the best knowledge about student learning" (p. 3). While principals cannot be expected to know everything there is to know about instruction and student learning, they must make every effort to keep up to date on effective instructional practices and encourage and support the faculty to implement these strategies. The principal must also be prepared to monitor and evaluate the instructional program, since we know that what is measured is what gets done most effectively.

Instruction is at the heart of the school's academic goal, but in order to be effective, it must be tailored to meet the needs of the students. Rick Ivers describes unique instructional programs that have been implemented at his school. Lori Musser emphasizes communication arts. Paul Young suggests that the importance attributed to mandated academic assessments can hurt programs for the arts. He reminds us of the importance of supporting the arts, such as music and art, to further enrich the lives and achievement possibilities for children. In addition, Gene Isenberg explains four very specific activities that work for middle school instructional programs. Others share specific instructional programs that include emphasizing best practices in the communication arts, employing a full-time writing teacher, reading ideas, and assessment ideas.

Special Instructional Programs

Rick Ivers
Alamosa, Colorado

Several unique instructional programs are used to improve student learning. One of the more successful methods utilized is the Literacy Lab. In the Literacy Lab, students in Grades 1 to 2 who are identified as being below grade level in reading receive one-on-one tutoring assistance in reading. This one-on-one instruction occurs four days a week, 30 minutes a day. The Literacy Lab utilizes two Title I teachers and two Title I aides. It has been shown that early identification and intervention for students is critical for these students to find reading success.

Another very successful instructional method that is utilized is having a full-time writing teacher. Our state assessments include testing in writing, mathematics, reading, and science. What we realized was that the mathematics, reading, and science components incorporated a significant amount of writing. To improve our state scores and overall writing skills, we use part of our Title I money to employ a full-time writing teacher. This writing teacher works with all students in Grades 1 to 5. The writing teacher works in cooperation with the classroom teacher to create lessons that utilize the best practices in teaching writing. These best practices include Shared Writing, Interactive Writing, Guided Writing, Independent Writing, and Six-Trait Writing. Having a uniform writing program teaches a common writing vocabulary and essential building blocks that are carried over to the next grade level.

A schoolwide two-hour literacy block that starts the first thing in the morning is also incorporated into the daily schedule. The first two hours of each day are set aside for literacy instruction. Distractions and interruptions are limited during this time, and all teachers work on reading or language arts during this block of time. Each teacher receives funds each year to purchase classroom novels for their classroom libraries. The school also utilizes Accelerated Reader and the Star Reader programs.

COMMUNICATION ARTS

Lori Musser
Joplin, Missouri

Communication arts are essential in the development of speaking, listening, language, reading, and writing. We address these areas using a balanced literacy approach to instruction through the proven Four-Block reading method. Students are provided whole group and small group reading instruction and often partner read with one another during the Guided Reading block. Daily activities strive to connect oral and written language experiences in order to help our students be successful readers. Teachers read orally to students on a daily basis to model good reading skills.

Phonics instruction and vocabulary words are emphasized during the Working With Words block. Students are provided many opportunities to apply what they learn to their reading. Minilessons are developed by the teacher to focus on specific skills. Each classroom has a word wall that contains commonly used vocabulary words. This provides the students with a visual resource so that they can correctly use these words in their writing and be continuously exposed to them throughout the year.

A Self-Selected Reading block is provided where students read books on their own levels. We believe that the best way to improve reading is to provide the students with a lot of exposure and experiences with reading, especially if the children are reading books on the subjects that suit their interests. Leveled books, library books, research-based textbooks are all resources used during communication arts instruction. Teachers conference with students about reading and writing on a regular basis during this block of time. We then track their progress using a reading wall that is posted in our teachers' lounge. We also hold biweekly literacy meetings. Accelerated Reader, a computer-based comprehension program, is used in our classrooms and focuses on students' independent reading.

The Writing block consists of many experiences with the children's own writing. Many keep journals, write their own stories, and write summaries of information that they have obtained through reading or write for specific instructional purposes as designated by the classroom teacher. A goal at Columbia is to help our students become confident and able writers. This helps them to be successful on the state-mandated Missouri Assessment Program (MAP) test. Proven techniques such as Power Writing and Writer's Workshop are incorporated into our writing instruction. Graphic organizers are often used as a means for children to organize their thoughts before they begin writing pieces. Writing rubrics are developed and implemented within our classrooms to dictate what quality writing consists of. This is an important skill the children need in order to be successful in a diverse and demanding society. Communication arts are integrated into every curriculum area, and children are active participants in instruction. Modifications are made for remedial and enrichment students.

At Columbia, our teaching practices are based on effective teaching strategies identified by Marzano, Pickering, and Pollock (2001) in their book *Classroom Instruction That Works*. Through research, Marzano and colleagues identified nine specific instructional strategies as having a high probability of improving student achievement for all students. This belief is directly related to our school vision and goals. Research shows that being good in compare-and-contrast activities is a top determiner of school success. Therefore, our teachers have incorporated graphic organizers, such as Venn diagrams, in order to provide maximum compare-and-contrast instruction. Our faculty studied Marzano and colleagues' book and in turn implemented the identified strategies into everyday curriculum throughout all subject areas. The specific strategies being used are recorded in the daily lesson plans. It is our belief that these strategies are one of the main reasons our students' performance and achievement have improved in recent years.

Teachers are encouraged to attend an abundance of professional development activities and are provided professional leave to do so. Teachers who attend out-of-district workshops return to Columbia and share what they learned with the rest of our faculty. This provides all of us the opportunity to learn from one teacher's experience. School-sponsored and district-sponsored professional development are provided. Teachers attend these workshops on designated professional development days when the students do not attend school. The professional development committee makes recommendations for workshops and provides assistance with registration and other arrangements. A specific professional development plan based on our school goals is established and followed throughout the school year.

Workshops already completed this year that pertain to our goals include a workshop on writing instruction, Working with Words instruction, and a bullying curriculum inservice. Our teachers attend monthly grade-level meetings where they learn about specific topics such as spelling instruction and improved math instruction. These grade-level meetings also provide a valuable opportunity to network with grade-level counterparts from other district schools. A team of administrators, teaching specialists, and grade-level representatives facilitate these meetings, and the focus is always directed toward effective instruction to improve student achievement.

New teachers meet monthly with the principal to discuss concerns and issues that are important to them. The new teachers share their ideas and common concerns as well as receive input and resources. The new teachers also meet with their mentor teachers on a regular basis to receive guidance, assistance, and valued advice. A two-week orientation titled Teacher Orientation to Promote Success (TOPS) is provided to new teachers in our district to help them become familiar with procedures and curriculum issues.

Principals Need to Support the Arts

Paul Young
Lancaster, Ohio

Fear of a poor performance on their school's high stakes testing is motivating many principals to carve additional instructional time out of an already jam-packed school day. Focusing more on reading, writing, math, and science, they often succumb to reducing or eliminating students' scheduled time in the "nonbasics." Children of poverty most often constitute the majority of students in "poor" performing schools. Unlike their more privileged peers, more often they don't have parental encouragement or support for afterschool music, art, dance lessons, sports, travel, or various club activities.

I enjoyed school because of music and art. I admired my music teachers, and they recognized and nurtured my talent, inspiring me to eventually pursue music study in college. I also sought and received special attention in art, where I experienced success and self-expression more than in any other subject area. I developed a lifelong love of running in physical education classes, and early experiences in student council sparked my desire to become a leader. These nonbasic experiences in the elementary grades had a lasting impact as my life interests and desire to learn developed.

So why would anyone in the principalship deny a child the same opportunities? It seems I argue this point with some of my colleagues all the time. Look at the research. Studies show that where schools increase opportunities in the arts for all students, test scores rise proportionately.

I know the impact the arts make! My Title I school consists of more than 60% poor Appalachians—a frequently neglected minority. Here is our story.

Six years ago, when I became principal of West Elementary School, the students, their parents, and community viewed their school with little pride—"tough west-siders with a chip on the shoulder." I assumed I was being punished when assigned there—that was the common assumption within the district. What I observed required change. The process and intricacies of the adaptive change process is a story on its own, but for now, let's focus on the arts.

West School's test scores traditionally ranked at or near the bottom of our district's nine elementary schools. I knew improving test scores would take time. There were too many other glaring problems: special education students in self-contained classes; angry and frustrated students, parents, and teachers; reactive punishments actions rather than proactive instructional discipline; low parental and community involvement; lack of pride and sense of belonging, and so on. To find something that could begin a turnaround, I relied upon the power of the arts—a constant positive within the school.

The focus was multifaceted: (1) acquisition of small summer arts enrichment program grants from the community, (2) integration of visual arts and illustrations with students' writing, (3) a music teacher who coordinated Music in Education lessons with all content areas, (4) development of an afterschool program supporting the arts, (5) creation of a code of conduct put to rhythm, drama, and visual displays, and (6) schoolwide dance, drama, and musical assemblies (I even played my trombone). These all worked together to begin a slow turnaround. Opportunities were developed to market these arts experiences. When the school piloted a program, the media was made aware, and the school community began to see themselves as pacesetters—with new pride. And all the while, the test scores gradually improved to the point that 2002 proficiency test scores ranked our students' reading the highest in Grades 1, 4, and 6. Scores over time consistently mirror the district mean rather than the bottom.

The arts played a constant role in the change process. The arts provided students reasons to come to school. The arts were an area where *all students* could experience success and renew their creative interests. The arts helped West School students develop pride and respect within the community, creating numerous opportunities for positive personal, often emotional, experiences with the school. A bad school has now become good. True to the research, the arts play a significant role in developing learning, particularly among children of poverty. And from the principal's perspective, through a long, often difficult, adaptive change process, the power and consistency of the arts became the pivot of that change: a more positive climate, renewed pride and self-concept, and higher levels of student achievement.

To those colleagues creating improvement plans at the expense of the arts—you are misled. Increasing time with the same reading and math intervention that students "didn't get" the first time will only get more of the same, as well as more discouraged students. They likely view themselves as failures. Those principals who schedule the nonbasics before or after the school day will deny equal opportunity and access to important school curricula, especially to the children of poverty—often that very group who see themselves as failures. They lack the means and parental support to elect before-school and afterschool offerings. And there is a diminished impact on the "hidden curriculum" and human interaction, obvious within engaged classes of learners, when the arts are missing. Closely observe a quality art, dance, or music class. Watch the learning, creative thinking, sharing, and socialization that occur—a valuable part of the nonbasics and all curricula. The arts will impact and improve students' self-image and their ability to accept and appreciate others. Why deny children these opportunities? Immerse them in the arts—where *all students* can be positively encouraged and enjoy success—and the interests in school and learning will come along.

I am proud of my staff at West School for their perseverance through adaptive change. One critical outcome of that change was the establishment of grade-level common planning time. Teachers meeting together weekly to develop and share lesson plans strengthened instruction throughout the school. And the arts were not neglected but rather encouraged and integrated in creative writing, social studies, and all content areas as appropriate. Our Intervention Assistance Team focused on students' strengths in music and art to find the key to open the world of learning to at-risk children. It's amazing how many intervention plans for troubled students, especially the hyper ones, focused on their interest in drawing.

What to do? First, remember that test scores reflect only one measure of a student's school performance. The arts provide essential, ongoing measures of the whole child. They also have a special ability to instill creativity, appreciation of diversity, problem solving, collaboration, and interpersonal skills—qualities as important for success in our society as the mastery of the basic skills. Children, like adults, are shaped by their external environments—academic, physical, and social (Gladwell, 2000).

When school leaders downplay the importance of the arts, they dismiss the huge role these nonbasics play in shaping who we are and how we act. Immersing our students in the aesthetic beauty and discipline of the arts, as part of each regular school day, especially for those who lack interest and motivation with the basics, is a better plan for improving school performance. Our schools will become community showplaces, our students will be more motivated, and the basics will be viewed with renewed interest and vigor.

Ramona's Triangle Speech

Ramona S. Trevino
Austin, Texas

As a firm believer in the power of the alignment of curriculum, instruction, and assessment, I began my days at Zilker Elementary School with what came to be known as "Ramona's triangle speech." Upon my arrival at Zilker, many parents were opposed to any discussion and preparation for the Texas Assessment of Academic Skills (TAAS), not fully understanding the state accountability system's purpose. As instructional leader, I set out to create a school climate focused on teaching and learning that emphasized a diagnostic approach. I began by building off the strengths of my staff. I keyed in on special education teachers, using their multitude of instructional practices as a model for regular classroom instruction. This soon came to be known as a teacher's bag of tricks from which an instructional approach was pulled after careful diagnosis of a student. It is imperative that teachers embrace each individual child and understand him or her as a learner. We discussed developmental theory and concepts such as learning styles and multiple intelligences. We studied

Ruby Payne's work on children of poverty and looked in depth at Hispanic cultural practices.

I created time for all teachers to be trained in annual planning and curriculum design. We began with math and soon worked on language arts, science, and social studies. We dissected the state Texas Essential Knowledge and Skills (TEKS) and re-created them into unified grade-level yearly plans. We discussed schoolwide assessments and committed to individual reading inventories for all students. From these results, service plans were created for at-risk students. A schoolwide portfolio system was established to assess student progress. Teachers were asked to do budget recommendations for materials that would support their instruction. Staff development became a priority, with individual plans outlined for each teacher and schoolwide standards established. Funds were allotted for national, state, and regional conferences, and teachers became leaders in sharing their insights and modeling implementation. Also, Socratic seminars were held to discuss issues ranging from poverty to aligning the spelling curriculum. Aligned philosophy statements and schoolwide standards were established for core content areas and for bilingual classes. The curriculum became public through open houses, curriculum nights, and displays of student work.

As a member of the Austin ISD Institute for Learning Planning Committee, I was actively involved in district implementation of the Principles of Learning. I soon became a trainer for my district in the principles of clear expectations, accountable talk, and academic rigor. Zilker became a site of frequent "learning walks," and as with all new initiatives, the staff were encouraged to re-create the concepts and make them work for their students. Our site was recognized as a model site for implementation and has been filmed by the University of Pittsburgh for a training CD and videotape on Accountable Talk.

BEGINNING WITH ASSESSMENT

Dan Coram

Wheeling, West Virginia

The mission and goals of Steenrod Elementary School serve to drive and weave curriculum, instruction, and assessment. Assessment begins, rather than ends, the process and guides the development of curriculum and instruction. Student performance is carefully analyzed to determine strengths, weaknesses, and developmental continuity. The curriculum is adjusted to meet the identified needs of the students from those who need more time to learn to those who need extensive enrichment, and teachers then develop appropriate teaching methods.

Several instructional strategies are common among all staff. First, the faculty recognize that learning takes place when prior knowledge is activated and regularly use processes of review and questioning techniques to capitalize on students' prior knowledge. Time spent on learning affects student performance; thus, teachers use every method possible to promote time on task. When individual students need more instructional time, teachers offer preteach and reteach opportunities. Basic skills are central to instruction and are taught in isolation, in context with one another, and with a part-to-whole emphasis. Finally, all teachers find challenging ways to address various modalities of learning and hold high expectations for every child.

In addition to these strategies, teachers employ other methods consistent with their individual teaching styles and the needs of their students. Such activities include direct instruction, hands-on discovery lessons, cooperative learning groups, projects, guided and independent practice, guest speakers, field trips, peer tutoring, intergrade-level activities, technology integration, and parent involvement.

Another strategy teachers use to add interest to instruction is the Steenrod outdoor classroom, a landscaped learning area. The Rhododendron Outdoor Classroom, called the ROC, creates the feel of a West Virginia mountainside. This allows students the opportunity to engage in the study of the flora native to their state, plant identification, weather monitoring, writing activities, and activities in art, music, and even math, which all enhance student learning.

Teachers recognize an instructional cycle of preassessment, topic introduction, time for practice, opportunities for application, and postassessment. They work individually and in concert with their peers and parents of their students to provide meaningful and efficient instruction to ensure mastery of basic skills child by child.

State Testing Is Fun for Everyone

Cindy Gipson
Raymond, Mississippi

Encouraging our children to perform to the best of their ability on our state test is an ongoing objective. On Meet the Teacher Day, teachers and parents review each individual test score in detail. Later, we have an Invitational Only awards program and brunch for family members of students who scored proficient or advanced in the three academic areas. Parents receive a formal letter in the mail congratulating them on their children's exceptional scores. During the awards ceremony, specially designed T-shirts are presented. The front of the shirt says our school name and "Top Test Taker." The back of the shirt has a star for each area in which the student scored advanced, giving some students up to three stars on their shirts.

Closer to testing time, we practice mini-sample tests and reward students with a special treat for excellent performance and for following directions. The day before testing, our *entire* staff grab pom-poms and conduct a pep rally. We have a great "Two Bits" routine, as well as an unbelievable dance routine to the song "YMCA." Instead of saying "It's fun to stay at the

Y-M-C-A," we say, "It's fun to take the T-E-S-T." Teachers form the letters T-E-S-T with their bodies. Results of significant test gains have been noted!

A Comprehensive/Diagnostic Approach to Reading Processes

Keith Owen
Pueblo, Colorado

Beulah Heights Elementary School has been involved in a partnership with the Lindamood-Bell Learning Processes since 1999. The purpose of the partnership was to introduce a proven clinical intensive reading model at the school level and provide intensive remediation to those students who needed it, based on a diagnostic battery of tests that are given to each of the children. With all teachers trained in our building, providing classroom instruction in the processes schoolwide became an expectation at our school. The use of a full-time facilitator to help our school throughout this process became especially important when we implemented this very specific program. Through the use of intensive reading groups, "pure form" reading instruction, and the integration of the reading processes across all content areas, we are moving forward in accomplishing our goal of having all children proficient in reading at their grade level.

Exemplary Instructional Practices

John Ciesluk
Longmeadow, Massachusetts

Principals place the highest priority on exemplary instructional practices. They are active in developing the school's curriculum and in carrying it out, working closely with teachers in determining effective instructional practices that are based on a thorough knowledge of research findings.

At Wolf Swamp Road Elementary School, it is critical that we have an aligned, spiraling curriculum and that we are using the best instructional practices that research suggests. Using the Plan, Do, Study, Act (PDSA) cycle, the school's curriculum and instructional practices are reviewed on a continuous basis to ensure that all students achieve at high levels. Teachers are expected to develop consensus curriculum maps that outline content, skills, and assessment. These maps are reviewed and updated at least annually, based on state curriculum standards and current research. The math and literacy teams have engaged in extensive work to lead the school in improving student mathematics skills and skills in writing across the curriculum. Recent schoolwide efforts have included helping students to be able to solve multistep word problems in mathematics and to respond critically and effectively to open response prompts in all subject areas.

All teachers develop an Individual Professional Development Plan that is keyed to the school's improvement objectives. Teachers are encouraged to attend workshops, courses, and summer institutes to learn about best practices. The school's PTO has been instrumental in providing supplemental funds to the school's operating budget to support summer institutes. Besides the traditional evaluation format assumed by the principal, veteran teachers are afforded opportunities to conduct peer-coaching projects.

Effective Instruction

Dawn Smith
Warm Springs, Oregon

Effective instruction is based on a common set of standards, aligned into yearlong teaching plans for each grade level and then aligned buildingwide from the lowest to highest grade levels. Instructional programs, then, are selected based on their correlation to the identified standards and a strong research base of effectiveness for the unique student population of the school.

Once the aligned curriculum is in place and supported by effective programs, common planning and discussion times for grade-level teams help ensure consistency in the curriculum delivery, pace, and implementation fidelity of the instructional programs. And, of course, effective instruction is only achieved with constant attention to assessing student growth. Assessment measures should be in place within the building to assess both individual students and groups of students on a daily, weekly, monthly, and yearly basis, and those measures of assessment should provide the leadership team, grade-level teams, individual teachers, students, and parents with quick access to achievement data.

IDEAS THAT WORK FOR MIDDLE SCHOOL CURRICULA

Gene M. Solomon
Upper Saddle River, New Jersey

"Framing Your Future"—The Arts/School Culture

During their three years at E. A. Cavallini Middle School, students maintain a sketchbook with drawings, poems, creative ideas, cartoons, designs, and other projects that they have produced. At the end of their eighth grade year, the students select their favorite pieces and create a poster-size framed collage of their work with their name calligraphied in the middle. At graduation, the students present their frames to their parents in appreciation for all they have done for them and as a remembrance of their time at Cavallini Middle School.

"Welcome to Ellis Island"—Interdisciplinary Unit

When the eighth graders dress in turn-of-the-century garb and, grouped by families, enter the Great Hall (the auditorium), they begin their own immigration experience in the Ellis Island Simulation. During the course of the day, students

- move through the processing center (the gym), where they stand in line to take a literacy test
- have their money converted (they need to be on guard for corrupt officials who may shortchange them)
- are judged by health examiners looking for disease or mental defects that might get them deported
- are assessed by customs officers who weigh their bags and look for contraband
- have their picture passports checked

To simulate the immigrants' confusion and frustration, almost no one speaks English to them. Bilingual parents volunteer as employees of Ellis Island. At the end of the program, tired, frustrated, yet elated, they return to the Great Hall and take the oath of allegiance to their new country. They then move to the dining area for an international banquet of ethnic food prepared by the students as part of this interdisciplinary unit.

"Lego Sumo Wrestling"—Technology Education

When the Lego Sumo Wrestling robotic vehicles compete in the ring to see which one is able to withstand the battle, students enthusiastically root for their favorite. This activity culminates in a Technology Education Unit during which time students, working in small groups, design and build Lego robotic vehicles. In addition, the students answer questions that focus on the principles of simple machines and gear reduction (which they used in their vehicle) and then assess the strengths and weaknesses of their design. This is just one example of how this hands-on, problem-based course uses tools and technology to teach students about the world around them.

"Dining and Dancing at Club Illusion"—The Arts

What better way to highlight the jazz band than by creating a jazz club in which band students perform. Each year, the school converts the multipurpose room into Club Illusion by putting red-and-black checkered tablecloths over student desks, surrounding them with bridge chairs, placing a candle globe on each table, and dimming the lights down low. Senior citizens are invited to Cavallini's Club Illusion, where they are entertained by the jazz and vocal ensembles while enjoying lunch served by the student council representatives. The following night, family and friends are invited to another performance.

SNAPSHOTS

Programs, Programs, Programs

Marla W. McGhee
Austin, Texas

We implemented best practice instructional programs such as Writing as a Process. We expanded assessments, including portfolios, rubrics, quality continuum documents, and scoring guides. We implemented reading recovery, reading workshop, and an outstanding library media program grounded in information processing and problem solving. These are just a few of the outstanding programs that we used to create a successful environment for students.

The Roll and Read Cart

Gloria L. Kumagai
St. Paul, Minnesota

In an effort to enhance student reading skills, we purchased nonfiction-leveled readers and a rolling cart through a $25,000 grant from a local business. On a daily basis, staff and parents and other community volunteers take the cart to classrooms where students check out books at their reading level. They take these books home to read with parents, guardians, or older siblings. Students bring back the books the next day with a signed slip indicating that they read the books at home. Another aspect of this activity is that teachers and volunteers also listen to students read part of their books before they check out new ones. After three years, families and volunteers continue to be very enthusiastic about the Roll and Read Cart, and students love taking the books home to read. The cart continues to actively engage students in reading and helps boost reading gains.

Readers Are Leaders

Sharon Roemer
Arroyo Grande, California

Readers Are Leaders is a reading incentive program designed to encourage reading for Grades 1 to 6. The program is sponsored by the Ocean View Elementary School PTA. Here's how it works: Tally sheets are sent home each month. Anytime students do any pleasure reading, they log the book and number of pages read on the tally sheet and turn it in to their teacher at the end of the month. Predetermined goals have been established. Once students achieve a particular goal, a prize is awarded. This is a fun program that encourages all students to participate. The program is voluntary and can be joined at any time during the student's time at Ocean View Elementary School.

Time With Students: Author's Lunches

Carol Loflin
San Ramon, California

Once a month, I schedule an Author's Lunch. Each teacher selects a student to bring a copy of something he or she has written to a lunch with me, the principal. The teachers, students, and I then sit down in a vacant classroom and eat lunch together while we listen to each student read a piece of writing he or she has completed.

At the end of each reading, we ask questions such as, Where did you get the idea for that story? What part of that story is fiction and what part is nonfiction? How did you go about developing that character? The children get really good at asking questions of one another, as well as of the teachers. This is a great way for students to know that their writing is valued. It is also a great way for the principal to get to know students as writers.

EFFECTIVE INSTRUCTIONAL PROGRAMS REFLECTION

1. What do I do to support the instructional program at our school?
2. How can I support the instructional program better?
3. What are effective instructional programs at our school?
4. What are instructional program weaknesses at our school?
5. Which ideas in this chapter do I especially like?
6. How can we implement these ideas in our school?
7. How might these ideas need to be revised to be successful on our campus?

ADDITIONAL RESOURCES

Accelerated Reader
http://www.mrstina.com/Areader.htm

Guided Writing
http://www.guidedwriting.com

Independent Writing
http://sg.sherrard.us/strandberg/independentwriting
.html

Interactive Writing
http://www.stanswartz.com/IAW%20excerpt.pdf

Power Writing
http://www.power-writing.com

Principles of Learning
http://www.Chlive.org/rpreisano/Principles%20of%20
Learning.htm

Shared Writing
http://www.sharedwriting.com

Six-Trait Writing
http://www.nwrel.org/assessment

REFERENCES

Gladwell, M. (2000). *The tipping point: How little things can make a big difference.* Boston: Little, Brown.

Hoy, A., & Hoy, W. (2003). *Instructional leadership: A learning-centered guide.* Boston: Allyn & Bacon.

Marzano, R., Pickering, D., & Pollock, J. (2001). *Classroom instruction that works: Research-based strategies for increasing student achievement.* Alexandria, VA: Association of Supervision and Curriculum Development.

School Improvement Plans

Never doubt that a small group of thoughtful, committed individuals can change the world; indeed it's the only thing that ever has.

—Margaret Mead

Fullan (2001) suggests in his book *Leading in a Culture of Change* that even though principals may be personally committed to new ideas, school reform, and improvement efforts, they are likely to be unsuccessful without the support and commitment of the faculty and others in the school community. Changing how things are done on a campus can be unsettling, which is why principals need to involve faculty in identifying campus needs and then provide professional training to support change efforts. This also increases the social capital of schools and strengthens relationships among stakeholders.

The best practice ideas in this chapter continue to emphasize ways that a school can improve. Scott Hollinger explains how book study groups can reframe the school community. Kim Boelkes describes how her school integrates the collection of data into its school improvement plan. Donald Greg Wood explains how his school uses the award process itself as an improvement process. Stephany Bourne details the best practices that enabled her school to go from failure to being an award-winning school. Other award-winning principals share ideas that include improving discipline, building teamwork, enabling teachers to visit other teachers, and encouraging teachers to understand their strengths.

Book Study Groups as a Tool for Reframing the School Community*

Scott Hollinger
McAllen, Texas

Your principal meets with you and announces that she is determined to get control of discipline. "Next year," she decrees, "all students and staff shall wear uniforms!"

If you support school uniforms, you'll be delighted. But if you're opposed to school uniforms, your principal's announcement will leave you nonplussed. You may respect her, trust her judgment, and admire her scholarship, but her announcement won't change your mind about school uniforms. You have developed your belief over time, and you will need a very good reason to change it.

Teachers are no different. Teachers who are committed to professional beliefs are not likely to adopt the principal's newest recommendation based solely on her declaration that it's a good one. Teachers develop their practice through real-life experience. Whether explicit or implicit, a philosophy of teaching and learning guides their work. Teachers' lesson

---

Author's Note: Reprinted with permission. This article originally appeared in the Summer 2000 *Texas Elementary Principals and Supervisors Journal.*

designs and classroom management are underpinned by their philosophy. A principal's suggestion that they try something different can be a direct assault on teachers' philosophy and practice. But a systematic investigation of the topic over time can change teachers' underlying beliefs. One way to involve teachers in systematic investigation is through book studies.

A case in point is Alfie Kohn's (1993) *Punished by Rewards: The Trouble With Gold Stars.* Incentive plans, A's, praise, and other bribes illustrate the point. Kohn teaches that our give-'em-a-sticker mentality has backfired by diminishing the intrinsic value of the things we reward. He says that rewards actually hurt kids and undermine our efforts. Many school leaders are now familiar with this principle and are encouraging their teachers to apply it in the classroom. But this thesis is heresy for teachers who believe behaviorism is necessary for education. And we see evidence of rewards all over: honor roll, perfect attendance, citizenship awards, pizza parties, stickers, and so on. A principal may realize that rewards are undermining the school's efforts, but her announcing to staff that "we're not using rewards any more" won't be sufficient to convince her teachers. If, however, the principal invites teachers to join her in reading Kohn's book over five weeks, she is likely to get the teachers at least to consider her perspective.

At McAuliffe Elementary School, one teacher began a study of *Punished by Rewards* with her arms crossed and her mind closed. "How can we ever get kids to learn if we don't use rewards?" she wanted to know. At our third meeting, she still wasn't convinced, but she was asking questions. At our fifth and last meeting, she still wasn't ready to give up rewards entirely, but she wanted her colleagues' suggestions for reducing the salience and frequency of the rewards she used.

The Book Study Process

In the book study process, 10 to 12 teachers read through a text over the course of several weeks. Participants meet once a week for an hour after school to discuss that week's reading. Each meeting begins with a silent review of the text for 10 to 15 minutes, then continues with 45 to 50 minutes of discussion. During the discussion phase, participants locate favorite passages in the text and share them with the group. It is essential that participants refer to the text when sharing passages. For example, "On page 72, the third paragraph says . . ." so that group members can follow the discussion and read for themselves the context of the passage to which the speaker is referring.

Ground rules keep the discussion moving and help to ensure that one person doesn't dominate. We use these ground rules:

1. Listen actively.

2. Build on what others say.

3. Don't step on others' talk.

4. Silences and pauses are okay.

5. Converse directly. There is no need to go through the facilitator.

6. Let the conversation flow. Don't raise hands.

7. Expose and suspend your assumptions.

8. Emphasize clarification, amplification, and implications of ideas.

9. Refer to the text and challenge others to go to the text.

10. Watch your air time, both how often you speak and how much you say.

Benefits of Book Studies

A book study brings the expert power of the text's author to your school. Along with Alfie Kohn, we've had Lucy Calkins, Irene Fountas, Gay Su Pinnel, and Ernest Boyer in our conference room just this year. And soon we'll have Stephen Krashen, Regie Routman, and Jacqueline and Martin Brooks too.

Book studies achieve more than just an investigation of a specific topic. Often, teachers learn that their current practice is not supported by the research. This creates cognitive dissonance. Allowing teachers to struggle with this cognitive dissonance is a constructivist approach to staff development. As teachers struggle with new ideas, they assimilate their new learning, scaffolding on previous knowledge, and push forward their zone of proximal development. This rarely happens in one-day lecture-style training sessions. Book studies provide an alternative to these "sit-n-get" sessions.

By studying a book over a period of several weeks, teachers have the time necessary to ponder their reading and its implications for practice. One third grade teacher at McAuliffe began a study of Lucy Calkins's (1994) *The Art of Teaching Writing* by stating that she already knew how to teach writing. By the third week, she was excitedly telling her colleagues how she had incorporated Calkins's ideas into her teaching and how successfully her students were writing.

Book studies help to establish norms of reflective practice among teachers. As book studies become a part of the school's culture, teachers are more likely to demand research before jumping on or off any more bandwagons. Book studies also dignify divergent thinking. It's okay, for example, to disagree with the text. But the teacher should be ready for her colleagues to ask her why she disagrees and what she proposes instead. Finally, book studies help to build a professional community and collegiality among the staff. Even if the group were to read Erma Bombeck, the act of reading, meeting, and talking each week would build camaraderie among the participants.

How to Plan a Book Study

The first question, of course, is which book to read. At McAuliffe, the principal selected the first several books. We began with Kohn and Boyer. Soon, teachers were suggesting books, and by the end of our first year, we were including titles in our Campus Improvement Plan. This year, we're reading Calkins and Fountas and Pinnel.

We buy 12 copies of each title and catalog them in the teacher resource section of our school's library. Each teacher checks out the book for the duration of the book study group. We encourage our teachers to mark in the books as they read. After a book study is completed, the teachers return their books to the library—although some teachers choose to buy their copy from the school.

Each book study needs a facilitator. The facilitator's job is to take care of bookkeeping, begin and end the sessions, and keep the discussion moving. It is not the job of the facilitator to lead the discussion or teach a lesson. At first, the principal, facilitator, and lead teacher strategist facilitated the book studies at McAuliffe. We wanted to model the process and set a professional tone for the sessions. As the number of book studies multiplied, we asked our teachers to facilitate. Usually, the facilitator is reading the book for the first time along with the group.

We usually hold the sessions after school on Mondays and Tuesdays, but we hold sessions on other days too, depending on teachers' preferences. We have held two book studies on Saturday mornings. The groups met at a local restaurant for breakfast and discussion. We give participants all the reading assignments at the beginning of the study. The reading assignments for Boyer's (1995) *The Basic School* were simple:

Session	Reading
1	Part I
2	Part II
3	Part III
4	Part IV

The reading assignments for Calkins's *The Art of Teaching Writing* were more complex:

Session	Chapters	Pages
1	1–4	1–52
2	5–7	53–108
3	8–10	109–182
4	11–13	183–230

5	14–17	231–286
6	18–19	287–336
7	20–22	337–368
8	23–24	369–430
9	25–26	431–482
10	27–29	483–518

Staff Participation

At first, teacher participation in book studies was voluntary. Now it's not. Two things changed our perspective. First, as more and more teachers participated in book studies of *The Basic School,* we became determined as a faculty to adopt *The Basic School* as a vision of our own school.

Eventually, we had to ask the few teachers who hadn't read the book yet to get in on a book study so they would understand our new common language. Second, as book studies became a part of our culture at McAuliffe, the faculty began to include titles in our Campus Improvement Plan. This elevated book studies to a form of staff development ratified by the site-based decision-making team.

Follow-up is an important element of this kind of staff development. We include blurbs about *The Basic School,* for example, in our weekly staff newsletter and our weekly parent newsletter. Every agenda of every faculty meeting and grade-level meeting includes a discussion of some element of *The Basic School.* This keeps the information fresh in teachers' minds and reminds them that our new learning is serious professional development, something different from the old "theme-o'-year" approach. When our school district used to introduce a new initiative each year, teachers could count on its being forgotten by the next year. At McAuliffe, we work hard to incorporate our new learning and make it part of who we are. Book studies have reinvigorated our staff development. And they have played a major role in reminding us that we, too, are lifelong learners.

Using Data to Improve the School

Kim Boelkes
Canton, Illinois

School Improvement Plan

Each staff member was assigned to one of four teams: Internal Review; Teaching and Learning Community; Student, Learning, and Progress; and Learning Community.

Internal Review. This team was responsible for surveying and interviewing staff, students, and parents about how they felt about our school. What changes needed to be made was a big part of this discussion.

Curriculum Alignment

We began by charting everything taught in each subject area by grade level. We then analyzed areas of duplication, areas not being covered, or areas where more emphasis was needed according to our state standards. A matrix was developed for each grade level, which included exit outcomes. Report cards were modified to include the outcomes.

Teaching and Learning Community. This team was responsible for assisting with new teaching methods that the staff had received inservice on. In addition, they developed schoolwide reading incentives.

Inservice

Data analysis indicated that our staff needed to work on reading and writing. Math skills could use improvement also. To master these areas of weakness, our staff was inserviced in the area of Four-Block Reading and Cognitively Guided Instruction (CGI) math. (CGI math informs teachers about how children think about simple arithmetic in the primary grades.) Training was comprehensive and ongoing throughout the course of two years.

Student, Learning, and Progress. This team focused their energies on analyzing data.

Data Collected and Analyzed

State test scores (all categories)

Achievement test scores

Reading level

Low income

Male/female

Absences/tardies

Teacher

Birth order

Demographic information

IQ

Number of parent contacts

Classroom grades

This information is added to an Excel spreadsheet. Color coding is added based on the following: excellent: green; average: blue; below average: yellow; failing: pink. Other items such as teacher, male/female are all color coded also. By color coding all areas, we can quickly sort our data to look for trends. Although entering data is time consuming, we have found this to be invaluable when it comes to finding where we need to focus our energy for improvement. Staff development, inservice, and allocation of funds are all based on findings from this data.

Learning Community. This team worked with community members and parents to review policies, look at what worked and what didn't, and make suggestions for changes to make our school a better place.

AWARD PROCESS AS AN IMPROVEMENT PROCESS

Donald Greg Wood
Wellford, South Carolina

At Wellford Elementary School, our mission is to promote the academic, social, and emotional growth of all children by providing quality educational opportunities in a safe, caring, and nurturing environment. We do this by our commitment to a continuous school improvement process. Since 2000, our school has been recognized with four prestigious state awards and two national awards. By participating in these six award processes, we looked closely at every aspect of our school. In fact, it is our participation in the awards process that has been the momentum for continuous school improvement.

In 1999, I asked our faculty if they would be interested in filling out the application for the Exemplary Writing School award. After discussing this with them and acknowledging the work it would entail and my support, I left the room so that the teachers could freely discuss and vote without my presence. Our faculty voted to embrace this challenge. We completed the award application, evaluated our writing program, and then our school was visited by an inspection team. Not only did our writing instruction improve, but we also won the award!

After being nominated by our assistant superintendent, we now had the confidence to apply for the Carolina First Palmetto's Finest award. Only two elementary schools in the state are selected for this prestigious award that looks at the overall school process and includes two site visits. We did not win the first year, but we did the next year!

As we filled out the applications for these various awards, we were directed to look closely at our programs and evaluate their effectiveness. At the same time, we began to visit award-winning schools to see where we could grow and improve. As we visited each school, we looked for procedures and programs and services to the community that caused these schools to be recognized for their effectiveness. Fortunately, we had strong district support in this process. Of course, as a faculty we wanted to be recognized for having strong programs and being a "great" school, but more than anything, we knew that this very act of self-inspection caused us to be a better school, and we are still getting better.

Now that we have had the opportunity to be recognized in these several forums, teachers and administrators are visiting our school. We now share with others what we are doing and why we are doing it regarding research, best practices, and academic performance. We also emphasize how we serve children beyond the school day, prepare for state testing, and the role we play in the larger community. This process of our becoming a "visited school" has contributed to our continued focus on school improvement as we strive to maintain the standards expected of a Palmetto's Finest elementary school.

From On-Review to Blue Ribbon School

Stephany Bourne
Ft. Wayne, Indiana

I have just completed my sixth year at an urban school with a population of 385 students that includes 64% economically disadvantaged students, 33% special needs students, and 21% ESL students. In the early years, we looked like this:

- No purposeful teaching or learning was going on.
- Discipline was out of control.
- Teachers taught and attended conferences in isolation.

- Parent participation of any kind was minimal.
- Staff, students, and parents were not held accountable and voiced daily excuses for failures.
- The building was dark, drab, and uninviting.

When the Indiana Statewide Testing for Educational Progress (ISTEP) test results came back for Indian Village Elementary School third graders in the fall of 2000, they scored a miserable 32%. Because of low performance issues, the state issued an on-site review. We were given two years and $20,000 in assistance money to reform our school and improve performance. In one year, we met the goals that we were given and were awarded the title Model School of Improvement by the state.

Six years later, we look like this:

- All regular education students have academic goals based on standards and are scoring (over the last three years) in the top region/state on ISTEP scores.
- Discipline referrals to the office are few in number; often we go days without a referral.
- Staff development is a top priority, and the majority of conferences are attended by the entire staff. It is very important that everyone "sing the same song."
- Parents, partnerships, and volunteer participation are at an all-time high. Around 97% of our parents attended this spring's parent-teacher conferences.
- We are a No Excuses! school. There is *no* reason why children cannot learn to achieve. We have the proof. High expectations for all prove to be key.
- Our building has undergone a $3.5 million renovation and is now warm and friendly.
- Poverty levels have remained stable.

Our school has experienced the entire spectrum of academic challenges, going from a state on-site review to becoming an NCLB Blue Ribbon School. We've managed to find success by

- Taking a personal and academic interest in all students
- Reviewing and using data daily to drive change

- Having all meetings be about academic achievement
- Building into the weekly schedule the time to collaborate
- Having teachers complete a Plan, Do, Check, Act calendar based on standards and implement weekly remedial sessions
- Creating a warm and friendly atmosphere where children feel safe and parents feel welcome

This has all been achieved through the Professional Learning Community process. Without this belief system in place, it is hard to imagine that any of this would have occurred.

INVOLVING STAKEHOLDERS IN SCHOOL IMPROVEMENT

Jane Hoskins Roberts
St. Albans, West Virginia

I would like to share an organizational method that is effective in ensuring that all staff and parent groups are involved in the development and monitoring of the school improvement plan. This structure also ensures that the school's budget and staff development plan are consistent with the goals of the school improvement plan. The process works like this:

Once data have been analyzed and the resulting school improvement goals are developed, a school improvement team is formed for each goal. Our goals typically fall under the headings of student achievement, parent and community involvement, technology, climate and safety, and character education. Staff members choose a school improvement team to join based on their expertise and interests. In addition to staff, parents who are members of our Local School Improvement Council join a team as well.

These teams each develop the objectives and the activities they feel will be needed to help us make progress toward that one goal. They also identify the *staff development or other resources* that will be needed in order to accomplish these activities. Once developed, the total plan is shared with the entire staff and Local School Improvement Council for revisions and consensus.

The chair of each of these teams now takes this process a step further. They form our curriculum team, and they have the responsibility of planning our budget and our staff development for the year. We also invite our PTO president to participate in this process. This curriculum team meets and each member shares with the group (about seven people are involved at this point) what *money* will be needed and what *training* our staff will need to accomplish the activities listed for their one goal.

In the process of developing the budget, teams meet for about four hours. Around the room I have hung a piece of chart paper for each type of money that comes to our school and the amount of money we receive. The charts typically include money that comes from the state, money from the county, and money generated at the local school level—for example, Title I: $8,935; Instructional Supply Money: $6,600; Library: $1,270; Staff Development: $3,300. Projected PTO funds and General Office Funds are listed as well.

As each team member reports on the needs they have identified, I record that need on a Post-it note, along with the money needed. Once all needs have been reported and listed on the Post-it notes, they are then placed on the various charts around the room, according to which account can be used for which need. Staff development funds obviously are used for training needs, and parent involvement activities typically come from Title I funds. We prioritize, subtract, and move Post-its around until we have reached a consensus that we have used our funds to help us accomplish our goals. Parents involved in the Local School Improvement Council and PTO see how their projects and fundraisers will be used to help the school reach the school improvement goals and objectives.

When finished, the school improvement plan, the budget, and the staff development plan are all coordinated, and everyone has had input at some level.

Making Time for School Improvement

Gina Segobiano
Belleville, Illinois

Signal Hill Elementary School is comprised of 36 full-time teachers serving approximately 430 students in kindergarten through Grade 8. Due to the district's small size, the luxury of having a curriculum specialist, a personnel director, a business manager, and other specialized personnel does not exist. Instructional leadership is shared between the superintendent and principal, and all teachers (two sections per grade level) are considered their own department heads. All school improvement efforts basically require all faculty members to take part and assume the role of curricular experts in each core area. The list of needed areas to address through school improvement efforts continue to become longer and longer each year. The same teachers and administrators are expected to tackle a wide variety of action plans, which encompass all of the students' social, emotional, and cognitive challenges that the district faces. The time needed to effectively address school improvement goals is spread thin, with limited opportunities for colleagues to spend quality time together to work toward reaching established goals. This scenario most likely reflects 60% of all school districts (i.e., rural and small districts) across the country.

The board of education at Signal Hill School recognizes the importance of establishing a set time within the school day for teachers to complete school improvement activities. For the past several years, the board has approved a school calendar whereby the students are dismissed 45 minutes early every Wednesday throughout the school year. (In Illinois, a full-day student attendance day must be at least five clock hours, excluding lunch and recess.) Though the vast majority of teachers spend extra hours on their own time to not only plan and prepare their instructional day but also complete school improvement tasks, the teachers are afforded a common time every Wednesday to collaborate with one another to work toward accomplishing districtwide goals.

The principal devises a Wednesday school improvement calendar for the year that identifies the purpose of each meeting as it relates to school improvement. The first and third Wednesdays of every month are dedicated to departmental meetings. The second Wednesday of the month is the traditional faculty meeting, where guest speakers or the principal may present an inservice to the faculty. The last Wednesday of every month is spent working on assigned school improvement teams.

Two times per month, the teachers conduct their own departmental meetings. The primary (K–2) department, the intermediate (Gr. 3–5) department, and the junior high (Gr. 6–8) department conduct separate meetings in order to articulate with one another. Each department designates a department leader who facilitates the meeting. In addition, another individual records the minutes to share with the administration for follow-up feedback. The first 20 minutes of every departmental meeting is used to touch base with one another on procedural or operational issues of the school day. Are the students too loud in the cafeteria? Are the students arriving to school on time? Are all parents responding to teacher requests and attending school functions? The discussion then leads to ways to address the problems identified. The last 30 minutes of the departmental meeting is used to discuss an educational topic relevant to the district's school improvement plan. Discussing ways to close the achievement gap, ideas to integrate technology into the curriculum, prereferral intervention strategies, or the implementation of the new Handwriting Without Tears program are some examples of discussion topics for teachers. The administration circulates and/or attends specific departmental meetings at the request of the teachers. The professional conversations held by Signal Hill teachers are invigorating! The teachers leave with enthusiasm and are refreshed and ready to tackle the challenges that lie ahead!

The second Wednesday of every month is your traditional faculty meeting. This time is dedicated to whole group inservices that interest all faculty members. Topics covered during this time would be crisis planning and emergency drill review, state assessment preparation, a special education topic such as ADHD or Asperger's syndrome, bullying, or a student management topic, and other topics as requested by the teachers. Often, teachers are asked to make a short presentation reflecting on key points learned after attending a workshop or seminar. The teachers show much leadership by sharing what they have learned with the faculty.

The last Wednesday of every month is devoted to team meetings. Each faculty member selects one school improvement team to serve on during the school year. Five teams are established and stem from the district's school improvement plan and/or strategic plan. This year, the designated teams are Technology Team, Character/Climate Team, Reading Team, Math Team, and Closing the Achievement Gap Team. Each team identifies two or three goals to accomplish throughout the school year. The superintendent and principal circulate and oversee the teacher teams. The teachers enjoy working collaboratively and usually leave the meeting with much enthusiasm and collegiality.

The Wednesday early dismissal meetings definitely improve staff relationships and promote a renewed sense of respect between one another—not to mention addressing school improvement goals. Engaging in a professional conversation is not only stimulating but also usually ends with an extension of learning by all teachers.

TEACHERS AS LIFELONG LEARNERS (TALL)

Scott Hollinger
McAllen, Texas

Teachers as Lifelong Learners (TALL) is a scheduling design. TALL time is a 90-minute period every school day when as many as six teachers can meet to work collaboratively. A different group of teachers participates in TALL time each day. While the teachers are working together, their students are instructed by PE staff. The PE staff plans enrichment activities for the children. Enrichment activities may include shoe tying for kindergartners, learning to play chess, a camping demonstration complete with tents, a fitness presentation by our district's health and PE coordinator, a student-oriented trivia game, landscaping work by the students, leap frog and other games, a numismatics demonstration, art activities, cooking, trading cards, kite flying, a presentation by the district's K-9 unit, and a field trip to the botanical gardens.

TALL time provides opportunities for teachers to work on curriculum, plan special activities, discuss students' needs, tutor students who need extra help, and administer individual student assessments. Each grade level has a joint planning period every six weeks. The Language Proficiency Assessment Committee (LPAC) and our school's prereferral screening team meet during TALL time too.

Our History in Extended Planning Time for Teachers

Ernest L. Boyer (1995), in *The Basic School,* points out the importance of team planning among teachers and concludes that "the key to team planning, of course, is time" (p. 35). "In the Basic School," says Boyer, "time is regularly set aside for professional collaboration" (p. 37). Many schools around the nation have arranged occasional extended planning time for their teachers. Some schools schedule extended PE periods for each grade level. Others carve out planning time by sending all the children from one grade level into other classrooms once a week. Still others hire substitute teachers to take over the classes on extended planning days. Our school typically hired half-day substitute teachers to relieve a grade level of teachers so they could plan collaboratively once each six weeks. With six classes per grade level, this arrangement cost us over $11,000 annually in substitute pay and "bought" us 648 teacher-hours for planning.

Where We Found Extra Time

The Basic School was a critical catalyst in our decision to use creative scheduling to permit collaborative time for teachers. It was clear as we read Boyer that we did not have the kind of collaborative planning time that he described. Historically, our PE classes were held in the early morning and late afternoon. During lunchtime, our PE staff served as recess monitors. We have now arranged our PE teachers' schedule so that PE classes are held continuously from 8:00 a.m. until 1:00 p.m. This leaves the PE staff free to provide enrichment classes between 1:00 p.m. and 3:00 p.m. Boyer says that "through . . . enrichment programs, the Basic School ensures that the educational and social needs of children are met" (pp. 156–157). We're covering recess supervision with playground monitors. We use the same $11,000 in substitute money to pay the playground monitors, but it now buys us a two-hour planning session every school day, for a total of 2,148 teacher-hours.

Early on, the school administrators scheduled TALL time. We used TALL time for grade-level planning, vertical team planning, tutoring, committee meetings, prereferral screening team meetings, planning of special cross-level events, curriculum planning, Language Assessment (LAS) testing, and Texas Primary Reading Inventory (TPRI) administration. Now teachers are clamoring for TALL time; we have more requests than we have days to allot. Meetings have better attendance. Discussion occurs at a higher level. Cross-grade collaboration occurs more often. Teachers' skills in collaboration have improved. Teachers are more apt to share ideas and are more action oriented. More and improved curriculum and instructional activities, including cross-grade events, have been the result. And back in the gym, TALL time is the ideal forum for presentations to students (poison control, fire safety house) and field trips.

Typically, each class goes to TALL time once or twice each six weeks, depending on the responsibilities of each teacher. Parents sometimes ask whether their children are missing out on instruction. Our answer is an emphatic "no." Our TALL time plan is much better than taking the teacher out of the classroom all day and hiring a substitute teacher. And it's great to be able to offer enrichment activities that we otherwise would not be able to offer in the curriculum. It's a win-win situation.

Best Practices Lead to School Improvement

Donald Greg Wood
Wellford, South Carolina

When our district reconfigured our schools to be primary schools with Pre-K through third grade, our district curriculum team looked at the research to create an ideal primary school that was more like a home than a school. This led us to follow research-based exemplary practices for primary schools. We created an environment where children work in groups and across grade levels. Brain research is considered in planning and in instruction, with special attention to developmentally appropriate practices. We use multiple assessments to drive instruction, such as running records in literature, benchmark testing, anecdotal records, and use of flexible groups to meet academic needs. Teachers set up academic workstations in their classrooms to provide children a choice in their learning.

In using best practices we have implemented two programs: Book Buddies and Communities. With Book Buddies, teachers team different grade levels of children together for reading and sharing. For example, third graders and first graders read together each week during the school year. Our curriculum facilitator provides instruction to the older children so that they can be more effective Book Buddies with the younger children.

Teachers at different grade levels have an opportunity to form a community. A community consists of a teacher from kindergarten, first grade, second grade, and third grade. The four teachers get together and each takes four or five students from each class. This means that a community might be led by a kindergarten teacher, but the students would be a mixture of kindergartners through third graders. Communities work together 40 minutes once a week with lessons focusing on South Carolina standards in science and literature. Every effort is made to include real-life, hands-on experiences for the academic topic. Last year, several teachers involved their community in larger community projects, such as visiting nursing homes on the holidays. Recently, on the first day of school, a parent shared with me that her child was excited to get a certain teacher because he had been part of that teacher's community in the past.

IMPROVING DISCIPLINE

Lori Musser
Joplin, Missouri

Our team of teachers noticed that the majority of discipline problems at Columbia Elementary School were occurring during recess, an unstructured and physical time. During school improvement meetings, a plan called Mustang Mediation was designed to help decrease recess problems and increase positive student interactions and make our school a safer, healthier, more pleasant place for our children. Mustang Mediation is a system of accountability and established consequences for violators of the playground safety rules already in place. During each recess period, teachers document playground rule violators and their offenses. A specific discipline plan was designed to address the students' violations of the rules:

- First offense: The student receives a written warning and verbal reminder of the rule;
- Second offense: The student fills out a "Think Sheet" on the rules broken and lists ways to improve; and,
- Third offense: The student attends the next scheduled Mustang Mediation at school.

During each Mustang Mediation session, the teacher, counselor, and principal discuss all three of the student's offenses, review the student's completed Think Sheet, and allow the student to present other information that relates to the offenses. After the discussion is completed, they issue an appropriate consequence for the offenses committed. Before the student can return to any recess activity, three things must be completed: He or she must return the mediation form signed by a parent or guardian, complete the consequence(s) given at the mediation session, and demonstrate full knowledge of all playground safety rules.

Mustang Mediation has been very successful, and six students have participated in a session this school year. This program provides the opportunity for all students to enjoy their recess activities without fear of being hurt in any way. Students are held accountable for their actions and required to make appropriate changes. This directly ties in to our vision and school goals by providing for the optimal development of our students' physical and emotional development.

TEAMWORK AS AN IMPROVEMENT PLAN

John Ciesluk
Longmeadow, Massachusetts

Principals recognize the importance of identifying and fostering potential in others. They are skillful in motivating others and creating a sense of purposeful collaboration among all members of the school community. Changes in the Wolf Swamp Road Elementary School's organization and important teacher leadership roles have emerged during the past few years.

The school community is characterized by teamwork at all levels, which has led to a mature use of the consensus model to consider school-based change efforts. As principal, I have organized the school into a series of teams designed to capitalize on the talents of all staff. Every teacher is expected to serve the school on at least one of its vertical teams and to make a positive impact to improve student learning. A Building Representatives Team of eight provides a voice for all aspects of the school in setting the monthly meeting agenda and channeling concerns to appropriate personnel for resolution. This same group plans the five Professional Development Days. The school also has a School Council that surveys all aspects of the school community and advises me on school improvement objectives.

Teachers serve as leaders of a variety of teams to advance the school's improvement objectives: a Mathematics Team, a Literacy Team, a Child Study Team, a Technology Team, and an Incident Management Team. All of these teams have representatives from every grade level, special subjects, and support personnel. The Learning Team (TLT) is charged with overseeing the work of the various teams as they address the school improvement objective. TLT is comprised of the chairs and the different vertical teams and teachers who assume roles as parent education consultant, Web master, and data and survey consultant. Success is measured by the ability of the schoolwide teams to operate in a self-sustaining manner.

Grade-level teams develop consensus curriculum maps based on state standards and plan instructional programs to address key skills, concepts, and understandings. Teachers with Professional Teacher Status are encouraged to engage in peer coaching in lieu of the traditional evaluation process.

Hiring new staff is an important role for principals who value a strong educational team. This important work needs to be augmented with mentoring to ensure that new staff members become integral members of the school community. At Wolf Swamp Road Elementary School, parent, teacher, and community input is valued when it comes to recruiting new staff. I form hiring teams to interview new candidates, and a consensus model is used to make recommendations about who is best to fill a role. Once staff members are hired, they are assigned a mentor in order to fully integrate their skills and talents into the fabric of the school.

TEACHER'S REPERTOIRE CONCEPT

Michele Pecina
Madera, California

One of my best practices is to encourage teachers to reflect on what is in their professional repertoire as a teacher. In other words, what can the teachers list in their knowledge of strategies? If the list is short, then more needs to be added through professional development. This is one way that we have been able to evaluate, as well as encourage, teachers to increase student achievement. Most of our teachers have quite a list of whole group, small group, and individual strategies, and they implement these strategies to meet the varied needs of students in their classrooms.

Previously, teachers went to workshops and (maybe) came back and used a few of the ideas. Monies are very precious today in our schools, but more important, our schools are being held accountable as never before for student achievement. If teachers are getting quality research professional development, the principal's expectation has to be that the professional development strategies learned must be implemented. We cannot afford not to give it a try and make a difference in the learning of students. Fortunately, what our campus has selected has given us a boost and students are doing better. Thus, a teacher's repertoire has been enlarged and there are more tools to effect student achievement.

SNAPSHOTS

Addressing the Digital Divide

Ramona S. Trevino
Austin, Texas

With a 50% economically disadvantaged population, I became passionate about addressing the digital divide. Our Blue Ribbon application clearly showed technology as our weakest area. I located a technology resource from a company called Learning.com. Zilker Elementary School soon became one of two pilot sites in the country to use this online resource at a limited cost to our school. Within a year, we became the model of technology instruction, with our annual plans now reflecting technology integration. I served on a district technology advisory council and a committee to align the technology TEKS (Texas Essential Knowledge and Skills) into grade-level curriculum frameworks. I passionately petitioned the district to purchase EasyTech from Learning.com and, as a member of the Partners in Education Executive Board, sold the idea of a curriculum resource for technology education to business partners. Effecting change at a district level was not easy but was very gratifying once my proposal was adopted and funded.

Teachers Visiting Teachers

Robert W. Fowls
Bend, Oregon

Periodically, we provide the opportunity for our own teachers to take a day or part of a day to visit other teachers in our school. The goal is for them to observe their colleagues doing what they do best within their own classrooms. It is an opportunity that teachers seldom get. This has provided an increase in sharing, cooperation, understanding, and appreciation for the members of the entire teaching team.

A High-Quality Teacher in Every Classroom

Keith Owen
Pueblo, Colorado

We are committed to providing the students at Beulah Heights Elementary School with the most highly qualified teachers available. We spend many hours throughout the recruiting and hiring process to ensure a highly qualified teacher for all students. We then take our highly qualified teachers and give them the tools they will need to be successful. We have put a professional development model in place that trains all staff in the use of scientifically based researched reading processes. Intensive reading groups are taught throughout the day and after school. Assessment of student needs in reading is documented, as all students in kindergarten through fifth grade have been given a complete battery of diagnostic tests to determine individual reading ability. After assessing each child's individual reading needs, we prescribe a course of action for every single child.

Steamy Summer Planning

Cindy Gipson
Raymond, Mississippi

Soon after the school year ends, our teachers return to school for five days for intense summer planning. Teachers work in teams to plan a comprehensive calendar of stories, units, and skills for the entire school year. State benchmarks are matched to individual stories, units, and skills for documentation of complete coverage of the state's expectations. When teachers complete the five days, the entire year's plan is in print so that all teachers will be prepared for success in the upcoming school year. Our teachers love this week! They believe that it is the key to the success of our students in moving ahead in reading, language, and math. As principal, I provide an agenda for each day to ensure that successful planning takes place.

Trashbusters

Scott Hollinger
McAllen, Texas

In the Dark Ages, picking up litter around the school grounds was a punishment for naughty children. Now, at my school, it's a privilege! Only third and fourth graders with good grades and conduct may fill out an application to be a Trashbuster. Parents must sign the application, and students must go through an interview. Those selected as Trashbusters work for a week at a time, every four weeks. These students are dismissed to lunch five minutes before their classmates. After a quick lunch, they use their own recess time to gather litter around the school, wearing an orange vest and latex gloves. The program is so popular that we have been forced to add a second round of applications for spring semester.

SCHOOL IMPROVEMENT PLANS REFLECTION

1. In what ways do I support school improvement?
2. In what areas am I strong in implementing school change?
3. In what areas do I need to improve?
4. What are school improvement planning needs at our school?
5. Which ideas in this chapter do I especially like?
6. How can we implement these ideas in our school?
7. How might they need to be revised to be successful on our campus?

ADDITIONAL RESOURCES

Asperger's Syndrome
http://www.aspergerinformation.net

The Basic School
http://www.boyercenter.org/basicschool

Book Buddies
http://kwr.co-nect.net/bookbuddies.html

Bullying (National PTA)
http://www.pta.org/bullying

Cognitively Guided Instruction (CGI)
http://www.discovery.k12.oh.US/03_programs/cgi_03.htm

EasyTech
http://www.learning.com

Exemplary Writing School Award
http://www.winsc.org/index.html

Handwriting Without Tears
http://www.hwtears.com

No Excuses! School
http://www.noexcuses.org

REFERENCES

Boyer, E. (1995). *The basic school.* Princeton, NJ: Carnegie Foundation for Advancement of Teaching.

Calkins, L. (1994). *The art of teaching writing* (2nd ed.). Portsmouth, NH: Heinemann.

Fullan, M. (2001). *Leading in a culture of change.* San Francisco: Jossey-Bass.

Kohn, A. (1993). *Punished by rewards: The trouble with gold stars.* Boston: Houghton Mifflin.

6

At-Risk Programs

Let us think of education as the means of developing our greatest abilities, because in each of us there is a private hope and dream, which, fulfilled, can be translated into benefit for everyone and greater strength for our nation.

—John F. Kennedy

Hodgkinson, in *Best Practices, Best Thinking and Emerging Issues in School Leadership* by Owings and Kaplan (2003), points out that "nothing is distributed evenly across the United States, not sex, race, religion, wealth, or educational level" (p. 5). He notes that in the year 2000, almost 50 million U.S. students taught by 2.4 million teachers could be found in over 80,000 schools. Even though one third of the population lives in only nine metro areas, 19,000 schools were located in big cities, 22,000 schools were in suburbs, and 39,000 schools were in small, rural areas. However, immigrant children and children of poverty live in big cities, suburbs, and in rural areas, and 10 million children attend a different school every year. Hodgkinson estimates that a million young people in the United States have no fixed address!

Hodgkinson emphasizes that considering the nation's complex racial, ethnic, and national origins "presents a challenge for educational leaders whose own diversity is thin and getting thinner" (p. 10). While nearly 40% of U.S. students are non-White, only 14% of elementary teachers, 10% of secondary teachers, 16% of principals, and 4% of superintendents are non-White. Added to this, of course, are myriad other kinds of diversity among our children that educators must address.

In order for school leaders to be effective, they must be concerned with helping all children achieve. This necessitates the creation and implementation of special programs to help underserved children be successful in the school environment. In our increasingly diverse society, these best practices must be embedded into the school day, whether children come from homes of high poverty, are limited English speakers, or have other needs. In this chapter, Elizabeth Neale and Mary Kay Sommers address how their campuses are championing the needs of English Language Learners (ELL) children. Carol J. Lark explains what her school is doing to create a safe learning environment through the use of choice theory. Other principals describe ways in which they are implementing programs that provide extra support to address the needs of struggling students in reading and math by being inclusive and using a variety of evaluation tools.

School as a Welcoming Center for Diversity

Elizabeth Neale
Pittsfield, Massachusetts

Even though we are a Title I school, we are a low incidence area of English Language Learners (ELL). However, the number of children who do not speak English is growing every day. Most of the children that we have who emigrate from other countries and who come to us not speaking English speak Spanish; however, increasingly, children are from Russia, Portugal, and parts of Africa.

The state of Massachusetts is still trying to decide what is best for ELL children, and for a long time, our district was not confronting this issue. This led me to ask if the ELL children could come to our school. Today, all the children in our district who do not speak English come to our campus.

We integrate the children into the classroom immediately. In addition, we have two ESL teachers. One teacher works with the children who speak no English at all. This is our Newcomers group. These children get special time to work on the overall adjustment to a new country. They meet other children who are experiencing the same needs. Our primary goal for these children is to help them feel comfortable in their new surroundings. As soon as they are comfortable, we begin to individualize their lessons as much as possible to meet their diverse needs. The other teacher primarily works with the children after they have some working knowledge of English. The primary emphasis of this class is literacy, and children have special time to work on phonetic helps, reading, and writing.

A big component of our success in working with ELL children is our Family Center. This is a resource room that is staffed by two AmeriCorps Fellows who are fluent in Spanish. This is a fabulous program! AmeriCorps is similar to Teach for America, but they work under the tutelage of others. We have been fortunate to have our Family Center funded by a special benefactor from the community.

Through the Family Center, we work with our non-English-speaking families to integrate them into the school community as quickly as possible. For example, we visit in the home and take a backpack filled with school supplies for the children. Recently, 100 computers were donated to our school by a local bank. Our AmeriCorps workers went into the homes to help set these up. Our Family Center also offers classes at night that include classes in English for new families to our country. There is no charge for these classes.

Our campus sponsors several Family Fun Nights during the school year. In order to encourage new families to participate, we keep these events very informal. Sometimes parents bring food from their diverse cultural backgrounds. We go out of our way to help our newest families attend, including picking them up! We have also found that parents are more likely to attend these group functions than come to the school alone. In fact, we have great attendance by our whole school family at our Family Fun Nights. This emphasizes the importance of the school as a welcoming community.

Our campus also has a school adjustment counselor (SAC). If a family comes to the school and needs help, we refer them to this individual. The SAC is able to help parents who need food stamps or who have housing needs. Families in need can be referred to homeless shelters or the battered women's shelter when necessary. If a child needs eyeglasses or clothes, our SAC is called upon to help fill that need. The school cannot do everything for children, but we do need to help when we can! In this way we establish a thick umbrella of trusting the community right away.

<hr />

What It Takes for a School of Excellence

Mary Kay Sommers
Fort Collins, Colorado

Shepardson Elementary School is dedicated to serving students with special education and ESL needs in a fully inclusive way. When hiring staff, it is important that they are comfortable with this model. Specialists work in classrooms with small, diverse, and/or flexible groups and train other staff and parents to provide small group or individualized help. Classroom instruction seeks to use differentiation methods to adjust to the differences in learning needs and styles. The natural result is a community of learners who respect each other for their differences and a staff who are dedicated to teaching students as unique learners in an inclusive format.

Our school has no special education room, for example, yet around 10% of our population has diverse needs (sometimes multiple-handicapped using assistive technology and, more regularly, students with Down syndrome, Asperger's syndrome, autism, cerebral palsy, brain injury, or dual diagnosis). In addition, we are a magnet site for ESL students (10%), most of whom are Hispanic, but our students use around eight different languages. Then we also have a large percentage of high achievers (we don't like to label them "gifted," but our scores, especially in math, tend to be very high, some years with over 50% in the "advanced" range).

I personally believe that the fully inclusive model using differentiation strategies within the classroom and with small, flexible groups best explains our success. The teachers who are committed to using this delivery model are to be commended for their hard work. We had five teachers quickly seek their ESL Endorsement upon our new magnet status as one way of explaining the commitment and dedication of this team. Staff development is sought both by individual teachers and by schoolwide or grade-level teams that focus on the school's goals and on individual professional growth plans. We combine the ESL and literacy teams, since the focus is the same, allowing us more flexibility to provide services directly to students in smaller instructional groups. Similarly, the special education teams serve a unit of students by grades rather than by disability (K–2, 3–4, or 5–6) to likewise create a more effective use of limited resources. What few paraprofessionals we have also serve to assist with small group or individualized instruction.

Parents are actively involved and embrace our diverse culture, even to the point of finding Buddy Parents the first year as an ESL Magnet site. We actively reach out to families who are not as comfortable in our school, and we will do home visits. We have two parent conferences a year: the first one is in the first few weeks and serves as a listening conference, where goals are set since parents know what they hope for their children, a conversation that enables them to become active partners in the process very early in the school year. Great success!

The second conference is an academic one, where the goals are described. Other conferences occur throughout the year as needed. The parent community, through the PTO, is exceptionally active in seeking more funds for us to use to expand our program (e.g., Homework Hotel, Afterschool Enrichment Program), expand a few hours of paraprofessionals' time, and provide assemblies, new materials, and money for staff to attend trainings. They also willingly volunteer regularly throughout the school and serve on leadership committees. Communication with parents is a priority, with school newsletters weekly in the first and last months of the school and on alternating weeks otherwise. We are fortunate to have a parent translate these newsletters into Spanish and another parent who maintains our Web site so they are easily accessible to staff, parents, and the community. Most teachers also communicate regularly, with more frequency occurring in younger grades.

The primary grades (1 and 2) are now looping to keep students for two years. All grade-level teams have joint planning time at least twice a week for 55 minutes to enable them to share strategies and frustrations and to problem-solve as a team. The arts are valued here and are not diminished for other academic purposes; however, the specialists are likewise finding ways to incorporate writing (our major goal) into their instruction as well. Music performances are integrated within the curriculum, and many students are given opportunities to share their talents and/or enthusiasm for the arts. The media specialist seeks multiple ways to integrate technology and media skills into the grade-level curriculum as well as find fun ways to generate high interest for reading in different genres. We keep seeking new strategies that not only increase student achievement but also provide relevancy and motivate each student to be an eager and responsible learner.

Our counselor is a critical part of our team and works closely with students, staff, and parents. He has initiated and trained peer mediators to help the younger children, which further enhances the Buddy Classrooms (K–6) that are focused on school goals and learning. He uses several programs from which to teach bully proofing, resiliency, and problem-solving skills in all classrooms. He is an active leader in understanding the barriers to student learning and mutual respect as well as solutions that address the diverse needs of our learners in a safe environment for learning and personal growth.

The counselor, along with several teachers, also sponsors an outstanding student council through which many fifth and sixth graders develop effective leadership skills. The student council actively seeks ways to develop a sense of community within the school while selecting ways to be philanthropic. Each year the council finds new ways to make this school, our community, or the world a better place. Last year, after listening to a father who had just returned from Iraq, students chose to do a shoe drive for the children in Iraq. Students are urged to help others, not just themselves. Last year, students also began a daily live morning announcement via closed-circuit TV as well as a Friday featured videotaped news report that often celebrated schoolwide events for students and staff. Students of all ages are given many opportunities to speak purposefully and serve in leadership roles.

Both the PTO and many of the staff provide enrichment programs to enhance and encourage enthusiasm for learning. We have around 70 students in Grades 5 and 6 who participate in choir; many students participate in District Field Days and will train with the PE teacher. The art teacher finds many opportunities to share student artwork within the building and the community as well as organizing a Family Art Night and an Empty Bowls Auction for the local food bank. The PTO funds a program after school that includes foreign language, science extensions, drama, chimes, physical activities, and many other creative classes. This program usually serves over 200 students during each session. Providing alternative learning experiences outside the typical day for both students and families is important to our school culture.

Sometimes students with ESL needs or other needs are given preinstruction to front-load for the language terms and concepts needed prior to classroom instruction. Sometimes we've had high-level students who need instruction using a contract due to our concern for their at-risk status. More frequently, we are able to provide extensions for students who have mastered the skills being taught within the classroom using differentiation strategies.

As a school, we use data regularly to not only determine growth in student achievement but also for the purpose of targeting instruction. Data are also useful in our summative reports as well as planning for future growth needs as a school. Staff assist with the goal-setting process and especially with the role they can serve to support these goals. Overall, we seek to help all children reach high levels of performance and avoid the stereotyping that comes naturally from subgroup data and focus. Keeping expectations high for each child, while holding each one accountable, are critical elements of our teaching strategy. We will continue to monitor all data and make needed adjustments, especially in those areas that suggest achievement gaps.

These are just some of the many and varied activities on our campus. In this way, staff and parents provide valuable talents and resources to ensure that all children are learning at their highest level.

BELOW-GRADE-LEVEL READERS

Lori Musser
Joplin, Missouri

Primary teachers conference daily with individual students to assess their literacy progress. Intermediate teachers conference weekly with each of their students. The diagnosis of the child's reading skills and ability produced by these conferences determines the teacher's approach to individualized and whole group instruction. The newly implemented Early Literacy and Reading Recovery programs are highly successful methods of reading instruction. Reading Recovery is an individualized reading program for first graders who are reading at the lowest levels. Students receive 30 minutes a day of individualized reading instruction focusing on the child's weaknesses.

The Reading Recovery teacher uses research-based practices and continual assessment to help students progress and improve their reading level. The Reading Recovery teacher also aids Columbia Elementary School's classroom teachers in developing and utilizing effective reading instruction. When students are reading at grade level, they graduate from Reading Recovery and another student is placed in the program.

Early Literacy is a small group instructional program that focuses on literacy. The Early Literacy teacher and classroom teachers work together to identify and assist students who have difficulty with reading and writing. It involves ongoing individual assessment of student needs, coteaching during guided reading instruction, and support in the planning and implementation of a balanced reading program. The lowest five readers in each grade are identified and receive specific reading and writing instruction with the Early Literacy teacher in a small group setting. This program was designed to provide all children, despite widely diverse backgrounds and abilities, with the opportunities needed to read and write.

First grade students involved in the Early Literacy program improved their reading level by 9.74 months during the first semester of the current school year. Second graders also made gains of 6.12 months. Twenty-nine Columbia students are being served through the Early Literacy program. A Literacy Wall was designed and implemented in 2001 at Columbia. The Literacy Wall displays the reading levels of all Columbia students and provides visible data for our teachers. Every student has a card placed on the wall under his or her current reading level heading. At a glance, teachers can observe a student's progress, or lack thereof, by the movement of the cards. Teachers move their own students' cards based on assessments and the students' progress in the classroom.

Columbia's teachers are interested in the progress of all of our students, not just the ones that they currently have in class. Teachers can often provide insight into a student's progress, especially if they have had the child in class before. The use of the students' initials and color coding, on the cards, ensures confidentiality.

We have also initiated a literacy team at Columbia. This team consists of the Reading Recovery teacher, Early Literacy teacher, the principal, and classroom teachers. The team meets every two weeks to discuss those students who are not adequately making progress in the areas of reading and writing. The literacy team meetings focus on teaching and learning issues, for example, administering and analyzing running records, planning constructive activities for literacy corners, and designing minilessons for a writer's workshop. These problem-solving discussions help Columbia's teachers with concerns they have about a student's progress and focus on meeting the specific needs of individual students. Good news and successes about students are also shared at these meetings.

Individualized reading improvement plans are another method used to meet our students' needs. Improvement plans are developed and implemented for fourth graders who are determined to be reading a year or more below grade level, based on the Stanford 9 assessment given in the fall. Columbia students placed on individual reading plans receive 30 hours of one-on-one tutoring after school. These students are also strongly urged to attend summer school in order to receive additional reading instruction. Classroom modifications are also developed and documented with the student's regular classroom teacher in order to help the student improve. Parents are notified and invited to participate in their student's reading improvement plan. Columbia has 10 students currently on reading improvement plans.

CREATING A SAFE AND EFFECTIVE LEARNING ENVIRONMENT IN AN AT-RISK SETTING

Carol J. Lark
North Las Vegas, Nevada

Having spent seven years as principal of a suburban school in an affluent area, I found that most of the discipline problems were fairly minor and could be handled with a parent conference and a behavior plan. When I requested an at-risk inner-city school, I was surprised to find that my previous strategies seemed to have absolutely little, if any, impact on improving student behavior.

My new school was 91% free or reduced lunch and 86% Hispanic. When I made the move, I talked 11 teachers into going with me, and after less than a month, they came to me and said that if I didn't get the behavior problems under control, they were leaving. When I sent the disruptive students home, pending a parent conference, they just came back stronger. If they wanted a day off, they just hit somebody. The parent conferences were often a total waste of time because the parents' problems were typically much worse than the children's problems.

I decided to write a grant to the state legislature that would support one of their recent bills (AB 521). In the grant, I funded one licensed and one support staff position. I also included funds for the training of a behavior team. I then sought advice from our local university and met Dr. Patti Chance from the University of Nevada at Las Vegas, who was trained in the William Glasser model of choice theory. She agreed to train my entire team and help us set up the program. We set aside two full days and went to my business partner's facility for the training. My team consisted of myself, the assistant principal, the counselor, a special education teacher, and several teachers from all grade levels (K–5). Glasser's choice theory model could be replicated in any school.

Choice theory basically puts the problem back in the hands of the child. It always boils down to the fact that we all have decisions, and every decision carries a consequence. The child is treated at all times with dignity and respect. The child is always able to make decisions to improve his or her circumstances. What the child soon learns, however, is that adults also have the right to make decisions that will impact his or her conditions. They are taught that at our school, no one has the right to disrupt the learning of others, and if they choose to do so, they will be removed from that environment immediately.

The real heart of the program is the behavior team, which meets every Thursday at 8:15 a.m. As principal, I chair that committee and someone is assigned to record the outcomes. We have a team of 15 because about 5 are always gone due to our being a year-round school and one track is always out. It is critical that the behavior specialist and a special education teacher be there for all meetings. As each child is discussed, that child is assigned two behavior team members, and the ups and downs of the week are shared. Essentially, each child "on the edge," as we call them, has four adults looking out for him or her every day. They have their classroom teacher, the behavior specialist, and two members of the behavior team. At each weekly meeting, each child is discussed and the past week's ups and downs are shared. Only one behavior at a time is targeted for improvement. The team shares suggested solutions. The classroom teacher often attends the meetings so that he or she totally understands the strategies being proposed. We never miss weekly meetings.

The history of the program reflects our progress. The first year we had 66 students removed from the classroom, and approximately 20 were repeat offenders. The second year 35 students were removed from the classroom, with 10 to 15 repeat offenders. The third year we dropped the support position because very few children were actually removed. We also were able to eliminate the need for a room set aside just for this purpose.

The role of the behavior specialist included meeting the students every morning and evening at the bus. His day consisted of walking in and out of all classrooms as a visible support to teachers. Throughout these visits, he would privately pull certain children to talk to them about how things were going and find out what problems they needed help with. He consistently communicates with the parents of troubled students and tries to guide them in some parenting skills as well. He never reports on teacher performance to me. He has established a high trust level with the classroom teachers and is viewed as support only.

The referral procedure is flexible. Teachers may refer a student to the behavior team by talking to the behavioral specialist or anyone on the behavior team. In rare cases, teachers may notify the office if a student is being disruptive, and the behavior specialist will be called by radio to go immediately to that classroom.

After about three years of the program, it was apparent that the entire culture of the school had changed. Choice theory had become a natural way of dealing with children by the total staff. We trained everyone in the basic language and philosophy, so we were all speaking the same language. When new students arrive, it is the peers who explain the program. Every child is treated with dignity and respect.

In the final analysis, only two children were sent home last year and none so far this year. The assistant principal and I do not deal with discipline outside of the once-a-week behavior team meeting. We are then free to be instructional leaders rather than disciplinarians. Choice theory is *not* a detention room. It is a total supportive team approach. A unique plan for every single child is developed and implemented by the behavior team and classroom teacher. We have a waiting list of teachers who want to serve on the behavior team, and they give up their prep time to observe and support their colleagues and the children. Once the program has been in place for two years, the entire culture seems to change. We have found that when the behavior specialist is gone for more than one week, the program starts to fall apart. I believe it is because these are high-maintenance children, with multiple problems, and no one else on staff has the time to devote to their needs. However, if their needs are not meet, they can wreak havoc on an entire school.

Thinking Out of the Box
for a Title I School

Orquidia Hathaway
Lake Forest, California

Six years ago, we were in a rut. Although we had half of our student population in an award-winning dual-language immersion program and the other half in an English immersion program, neither program was making the level of improvement that truly made the school an achieving school, despite small increments in growth. Our state had recently adopted extremely rigorous standards for learning in every curricular area. As a Title I school with almost half our population learning English and more than that socioeconomically disadvantaged, the stakes were enormous. Either we met the performance growth set annually or failed and experienced the consequences.

We had to find new ways to serve the growing at-risk population and help the children improve academically. The answer was to think out of the box and restructure our programs. We could no longer afford to conduct business as usual. The process began with the staff developing a set of beliefs that led to a mission and vision that served our growing at-risk population. We stopped teaching a classroom and began teaching a grade level. We stopped teaching a set of lessons and began teaching curricular standards to all children. We stopped making excuses for children's inabilities and focused on building children's strengths. In other words, we reengineered the process to deliver instruction at the child's level while still delivering the required standards at each grade level. The results were as follows:

- The children at every grade level became everyone's children (no more individual classroom instruction or, as we called them, isolated islands in the ocean).
- The teachers at each grade level became pals, planned together without involving "planned sessions," and shared best practices at and across the grade levels.
- The students were grouped for part of their reading and math instruction with one teacher who was responsible for delivering the standards-based lesson at their level (at, below, and above grade level, including gifted students).
- All grade levels timelined their outcome standards so that all students, by the end of the school year, regardless of ability level, received appropriate instruction in every standard.
- Students were assessed and moved as necessary from one group to another, based on progress, every four to five weeks.
- We developed an extensive longitudinal database of student performance (now five years old).
- We based all curriculum changes and student grouping on data.
- Teachers received training and implemented data analysis to plan instruction annually.
- Student performance rose dramatically annually for every subgroup, resulting in every award possible (State Distinguished School, Title I Achieving School, School Boards Association Golden Bell Program award, and National Blue Ribbon award in a period of three years).
- The challenge goes up a notch as NCLB requirements escalate for a school like ours. We are ready!

Inclusion of All Students

John Ciesluk
Longmeadow, Massachusetts

"All students belong" and "eyes on the child learning" are mottos that are lived out at Wolf Swamp Road Elementary School by the school's staff on a daily basis. Whether the student comes to us with Down syndrome, autism, Asperger's syndrome, or a major behavioral disorder, students are welcomed. They don't need to earn a sense of belonging.

Not only do students join in with other students in a regular classroom, but they take on special roles that allow them to contribute to the school in special ways. Students diagnosed with speech disorders lead the morning announcements. Two years ago, a Down syndrome student learned to read at a primer level at the end of second grade. His parents consented to having a videotape made of his progress and permitted it to be shared with others so they could see what is possible when we truly believe that all students can be successful learners.

In addition, beforeschool and afterschool enrichment programs have been developed and are available on a competitive fee basis. These are coordinated through the Parks and Recreation Commission.

Snapshots

Services for Struggling Students

Lori Musser
Joplin, Missouri

A referral is made to our intervention team by a struggling student's teacher or parent identifying specific concerns. Strategies are devised and implemented by the team in an attempt to help the student improve. If after two weeks the child is not showing improvement, a diagnostic evaluation is performed to pinpoint the student's specific deficits. Individual planning then takes place and objectives are identified for the student. The team consists of the parent, classroom teacher, special education teacher, counselor, administrator, and other pertinent staff members.

Individual counseling, peer tutoring, social skills instruction, preferential seating, utilization of outside resources such as the division of family services, parent involvement, and functional behavior assessments are some of the interventions implemented for our struggling students. Special education services are provided by well-trained resource teachers, classroom paraprofessionals, and other staff members. The program and services are based solely on the student's specific needs and are continually monitored.

STAR Reading Program

Sharon Roemer
Arroyo Grande, California

Ocean View Elementary School has one full-time and one half-time tutor. Students are referred by their teachers. They are given extensive diagnostic testing by the tutors and receive one-on-one reading instruction for 30 minutes daily. Reading tutors are certified teachers who have been trained in the reading process. An important component of STAR is to involve parents, who attend the tutoring sessions and learn specific skills to use at home with their children on a daily basis. This program accepts students from the second grade for the first semester and then first grade students during the latter part of the school year.

Extended Day Intensive Reading Clinics

Keith Owen
Pueblo, Colorado

We knew that we needed more time with our students if we were going to have an impact on their reading ability. We wrote a state grant under Read to Achieve and have run intensive afterschool reading groups for an hour each day with our second and third grade students who are behind in reading. We have each of our certified teachers sign up for a quarter each year, and they work with the students in groups of five to one. We are entering our fourth year in this approach. We have seen fantastic results in our reading achievement and have used this model as professional development for all of our staff each year. Parents have really supported this opportunity for their children and have provided transportation to many of the students involved.

Afterschool Math and Reading Clubs

Lori Musser
Joplin, Missouri

Third-, fourth-, and fifth-grade students who are below grade level in math and/or reading by the Stanford 9, Missouri Assessment Program, and classroom performance attend the afterschool clubs. The clubs meet one day a week, after school for one hour, and focus on students' weaknesses. The classes are taught by some of our certified teachers. Students receive additional activities and small group instruction in curriculum objectives on their level. Hands-on activities, group projects, and manipulatives are regularly utilized to help students develop critical thinking and problem-solving skills and apply these skills to real-life situations.

Provide Every Student Opportunity

Lori Musser
Joplin, Missouri

Our mission at Columbia Elementary School is to give each student the opportunity to advance at a maximum individual rate intellectually, physically, socially, and emotionally in order to be appropriately prepared to meet a multitude of challenges in our changing society. The last couple of years have seen a revision in the way that teachers are teaching at Columbia. Low test scores in state-assessed areas led us to do a dramatic self-study and intensely look at our teaching practices. At Columbia, we have adopted more effective, research-based teaching strategies based on students' specific needs and weaknesses to improve the achievement of Columbia's students.

Even an Opera

Marla W. McGhee
Austin, Texas

One example of an at-risk program at Live Oak Elementary School was a collaboration with the Austin Lyric Opera. The at-risk and latchkey kids at Live Oak and the music teacher, Kathy Smith, wrote and performed an opera about the community, or Jollyville, where Live Oak is located. It was fabulous! I stood in the back of the cafeteria and cried my eyes out when I watched the performance—I was so proud of our kids and staff!

We also had a premier special education program with a true continuum of services, from full inclusion to specific one-on-one instruction for those who needed it. We had a fantastic learning lab for both special education students and any student in need of assistance.

AT-RISK PROGRAMS REFLECTION

1. How diverse is our student population?
2. How diverse is our faculty?
3. What are at-risk program strengths at our school?
4. What are at-risk program needs at our school?
5. Which ideas in this chapter do I especially like?
6. How can we implement these ideas in our school?
7. How might they need to be revised to be successful on our campus?

ADDITIONAL RESOURCES

AmeriCorps
http://www.americorps.org

Choice Theory
http://www.wglasser.com

Early Literacy
http://www.ciera.org

Looping
http://www.eric.uoregon.edu/publications/digests/digest
123.html

Peer Mediation
http://www.teachersfirst.com/lessons/mediate/mediate1
.html

Reading Recovery
http://www.readingrecovery.com

Read to Achieve
http://www.nba.com/features/rta_index.html

REFERENCE

Owings, W. A., & Kaplan, L. S. (Eds.). (2003). *Best practices, best thinking and emerging issues in school leadership.* Thousand Oaks, CA: Corwin.

7

Other Helpful Hints

The best educated human being is the one who understands most about the life in which he is placed.

—Helen Keller

In addition to emphasizing best practices in leadership, shaping campus culture, collaborating and communicating, providing effective instructional programs, implementing school improvement plans and at-risk programs, principals have best practice ideas that help them be viewed as effective principals in general. An important consideration for principals is how to build their own knowledge base, and Gina Segobiano provides helpful suggestions to encourage principal learning. Instead of a Snapshots section at the end of this chapter, I have included a section on general wellness ideas. Acknowledging the demanding role of the principalship, several principals give advice about how to live healthy, balanced lives, professionally and personally. Karen Lyon even includes a blueprint for staff development featuring wellness.

BUILDING A KNOWLEDGE BASE

Gina Segobiano
Belleville, Illinois

Principals who serve a broad range of grade levels tend to feel the pressure of needing to educate themselves not only on the latest educational issues and trends but also on the research that supports best practices of instructional programs for the core areas. The core and related areas that an instructional leader should be proficient in would be reading, language arts, math, social sciences, sciences, fine arts, technology, character education, early childhood, special education, gifted, diverse learners—not to mention leadership, parent involvement, multiple intelligences, mentoring new teachers, and ways to close the achievement gap. The list could go on and on. To some, that task might seem attainable; for others, overwhelming. As the educational leader of a K–8 school, I can attest that the stack of educational journals and professional books sitting next to my bed only seem to get higher and higher. It is impractical to think one can keep up with the reading required to build a knowledge base on all topics.

Principals do not have to be an expert in every area. Principals, however, should be able to conduct a professional conversation with teachers and parents on various educational topics and should also develop opinions based on research and personal beliefs and experiences. By familiarizing themselves with a wide variety of educational topics that can be communicated to interested parties, principals will gain respect among the faculty, parents, superintendent, and board members.

It is important for every educator to set aside a time each night for reading. Personally, I allocate at least one hour for reading every night before I go to bed. Prioritize your reading by selecting journals or professional books that directly relate to issues that are faced within your district. When you come across a meaningful article, share it with your colleagues and staff or present the information at the next faculty meeting.

Let your teachers know that you too keep up with reading various articles to improve your knowledge base. Hopefully, your teachers will follow your example and will take the initiative to read educational books and articles to improve their own knowledge base.

Another avenue to gain important information is to become a member of your state association as well as a national association. Membership in various associations will provide an educator with relevant educational, up-to-date material and will also foster networking opportunities within your region or state. By attending state or national conventions, an administrator can gain a wealth of immediate information, plus be exposed to nationally known speakers in the field of education. The various individuals one can meet at conferences can result in long-lasting friendships that end up serving as a principal's support system. Do not be afraid to serve on one of the state association's committees. Involvement at the state level and even national level will only enhance one's leadership.

At times, administrative positions can be very lonely. Usually, there is only one principal at the building or even in the district as a whole. It is important to network with other administrators in the area to share common problems or to reflect on effective practices. One can learn a lot from colleagues, but it takes one to initiate the meeting date and time. The area principals in my area formed a networking group and called themselves the B.A.AD. group (Belleville Area Administrators). The group met once a month after school with a twofold purpose: to share common frustrations and situations that need advice and to socialize. The group of principals grew each year, and now even superintendents attend!

Administrators are definitely lifelong learners. Take advantage and build your knowledge base. When you feel confident with the material, spread the word to others—it's contagious!

CONTINUED STAFF DEVELOPMENT

Gloria L. Kumagai
St. Paul, Minnesota

Remember to provide for your own professional development as a principal. Too many times principals do not take advantage of the professional development that might be offered by the district and through professional associations and other organizations. It is just so easy to become isolated in our very own buildings!

EGALITARIAN PARKING

Gene M. Solomon
Upper Saddle River, New Jersey

I always say the key to a principal's success can be summarized in two words: "egalitarian parking." All parking spots, including the principal's, should be on a first come, first served basis. Why should a principal get a closer parking space than the sixth grade teacher who comes in extra early? It may seem mundane, but the teachers were very happy when this practice was implemented.

NO INTERRUPTIONS!

Ursina Swanson
St. Louis Park, Minnesota

I stringently protect class time and do not allow any interruptions during instructional time. There are just too many valuable things for us to accomplish that are all about academics and teaching and learning. No announcements are made over the intercom, so that teachers are not interrupted while they teach.

Involving Stakeholders

Donald Greg Wood
Wellford, South Carolina

When we make sure that faculty members have the same information that administrative staff have, quality teachers make quality decisions. Whether the decisions are about program processes or procedures, their decisions are effective and are as good as or better than our administrative team's decisions. When faculty are involved in decisions at the building level, they will feel our trust as leaders while supporting the decisions that are made by their peers. Shared decision processes are an important part of creating an effective school.

Teachers Teaching Teachers

Donald Greg Wood
Wellford, South Carolina

We want our teachers to be creative, and we encourage them to learn from each other. We have a Wellford Elementary School Saturday Academy on the third Saturday in January, just before Martin Luther King Jr. Day. The academy meets from 9 to 12 in the morning. Selected teachers are invited to prepare one-hour miniworkshops to share with other teachers. There are three sessions, so teachers or teams of teachers present two sessions and attend another session. We give teachers comp time for attending and for preparing a miniworkshop. We invite K–3 teachers from throughout our district as well as senior education majors from four local colleges and universities to our academy. This makes a great recruitment tool!

PLEASURABLE PERKS

Scott Hollinger
McAllen, Texas

Each year, we hold one or two faculty meetings off campus at a local restaurant, where we conduct our school business while sitting around tables and eating appetizers that I pay for. Twice a year, we invite the local cosmetology school to send students to give our teachers manicures. The students get practice hours and the teachers get free manicures. I give the cosmetology school a small check to say thanks. Twice each year, I pay for a massage therapist to give neck and shoulder massages during teachers' conference periods. Near the holidays, I give teachers a packet with coupons such as "lesson plans late" and "leave school 30 minutes early." (When using the coupons would leave students unsupervised, the teachers have to arrange to have another professional staff member take the class.) Finally, the school buys a T-shirt for every staff member every year, and we have our group picture taken wearing the T-shirt. (Don't forget to include the secretaries, custodians, cafeteria workers, and itinerant staff!)

TO A NEW PRINCIPAL

Elizabeth Neale
Pittsfield, Massachusetts

Be a huge listener and a huge visitor in the classrooms! Establish a sense of being available and visible quickly. Do *not* wait too long to visit in classrooms. Instead, establish that you are a part of the classroom. If you wait too long, you will likely feel like an interloper the rest of the year. Being visible helps principals seem less threatening to the faculty.

WELLNESS FOR EVERYONE

Karen Lyon
DeLand, Florida

This year, I am concentrating on a wellness program for the entire staff. We will begin on a preservice day and take the whole morning to introduce and implement wellness concepts and techniques to the faculty. A sample morning schedule looks something like this:

9:00–9:15   When teachers arrive, have fruit, juices, nuts, and water. Provide everyone with a stress ball. Call out names before throwing the ball across the room for them to catch. Give everyone a pedometer and encourage its use every day.

9:15–9:30   Discuss motivation for getting and staying healthy and how this affects attitudes, eating habits, exercising, and investing in good nutrition.

9:30–9:40   Discuss the concept of Kingdom Wellness (adapted from D. A. Ardell, 1988).

9:40–10:10   Complete the six activities in six different locations to get everyone moving. The activities will give each team member the opportunity to experience the hidden power of intention, building rapport, a sense of joy and wonder, belonging, taking risks and modeling clear communication, great listening, and reframing negative situations to find the positive in them.

10:10–10:20 Teams return and add up the teams' total steps walked; talk about how each individual's stride is different.

10:20–10:40 Debrief activity. Focus on the physical, emotional, intellectual, social, spiritual.

10:45–11:30 Continue discussion of Kingdom Wellness (includes natural motivations, personality types, learning more about self).

11:35–11:55 Discuss how personalities respond to stress management, dieting, exercise, balancing health issues.

12:00–12:15 Develop personal wellness plan. Discuss short-term goal setting and time management.

12:15–12:50 Time for celebrating opportunity to commit and persevere toward Kingdom Wellness.

To enhance the commitment to wellness, in addition to the pedometers for each teacher, we also purchased a massage chair for the teachers' room. We will continue to follow up with the idea of wellness at each faculty meeting by doing some stretching and walking before the faculty meeting begins to encourage all teachers to stay on track with their personal plan.

◆

Maintain Your Sanity

Linda Webb
Austin, Texas

Take care of the important things—your sanity and your family—and insist that your teachers do the same. I played golf on Friday after work. I would stay as late as I needed to during the week, but on Fridays I left at 4:00 to play golf.

Having this time set aside for me helped me get through those long hours during the rest of the week.

I also insisted that teachers take care of themselves. If they had a sick child, I insisted that they stay home with their child. I approved all personal days and encouraged teachers to take some time for themselves. Remember, people cannot take care of others if they do not take care of themselves.

One more thing: Read anything that makes you laugh, because you have to keep your sense of humor!

BALANCE

Mary Kay Sommers
Fort Collins, Colorado

Keep a balance (although I don't always do this so well). Watch the FISH video and try to incorporate fun into your culture. Everyone needs to have stress at a reasonable level, and humor is critical. Try to stay organized and keep effective to-do lists so you don't have to remember everything—you will be able to relax more when your systems are in place.

FAMILY COUNTS

Kathleen Genovese Haworth
North Hollywood, California

At the end of the day, it's your family that counts. As much as these positions demand 24-7, don't let daily issues take priority. If you need to bring work home, schedule undivided time with your children and spouse. It is surprising how solutions just pop into your head once you release them for a bit!

TAKE CARE OF YOURSELF

Cynthia Eliser
Raceland, Louisiana

I feel that many people lose sight of taking care of themselves. I hear many people say they don't have time to do fun things. We find time for what we think is important.

Being a principal is an awesome, exciting job! Days go by so quickly because there is never a moment of boredom on a school site. I have been a principal for nine and one-half years and have a passion for my work.

School site administrators work long hours and have many, many responsibilities dealing with *everyone* (students, parents, families, teachers, custodians, bus drivers, clericals, itinerants, cooks, supervisors, the superintendent, community persons, etc.). Federal, state, and local laws and practices must be a focal point of every moment of the day. Time management is a must!

The *best general advice* that I can give to anyone with such a demanding position is never to lose focus of who is number one. *Oneself*! I would suggest developing a hobby or a practice that you really like and schedule time for it regularly. I live in South Louisiana, where people use the phrase "Laissez les bon temps roulez." This translates to "Let the good times roll." As serious and professional as I am on my job, I can relax when I am doing what I love to do for fun—Cajun and zydeco dancing! While dancing with my husband in Louisiana dance halls and festivals to the rhythms of the accordion, fiddle, drum, and scrub board, I sometimes look up and say, "What school?" That's how relaxed I get!

We dance every weekend. When out dancing, I often meet new people, and we converse about where we work. When I say that I'm a school principal, people often say, "You don't look like a principal out there dancing!" My reply is, "Do you know what your principal looks like on weekends? I only hope your principal is out having fun somewhere too." On Monday, I go back to work, rejuvenated and ready to face the new week.

I would suggest to every principal that you take time to enjoy what you like to do. You cannot take care of anyone else if you do not take care of yourself. Don't ever say that you do not have time to do what you enjoy. I hear people say this over and over. Life is precious. Make time for yourself. The school will exist long after you are gone. Remember, "Laissez les bon temps roulez." Find a hobby if you don't have one. Remember, if you don't take care of yourself, no one else will!

Relax

Rod Smith
Lenexa, Kansas

One of my favorite ways to relax and unwind is to drive to the local trout stream, put on my waders, and stand in the beautiful, relaxing stream and fish for trout. Taking my family to an apple orchard to pick apples is also great therapy and so much fun. Lots of exercise and good nutrition always help.

Be Energetic and Well Rounded

Elizabeth Neale
Pittsfield, Massachusetts

Principals must do it all. You can't be a good principal without being superprincipal! It's sort of like the supermom or superdad syndrome. Good principals keep up a high level of energy. While it's impossible to attend every activity on your campus, you should make efforts to try to attend as much as possible. Sometimes you can just stop by to see what's going on and need not stay for the entire activity. This demonstrates that you're interested.

At the same time, you must be really well rounded. This means there must be more to your life than being a principal. You need friends to let off steam. It's important to try to do a bit of everything to keep you from being one-dimensional.

OTHER HELPFUL HINTS REFLECTION
1. What professional advice would I give to another principal?
2. What personal advice would I give to another principal?
3. What professional advice in this chapter would help me the most?
4. What personal advice in this chapter would help me the most?
5. How can I implement these ideas in my life?
6. How might these ideas need to be revised?

REFERENCE

Ardell, D. A. (1988). *Planning for wellness: A commitment to personal excellence.* Dubuque, IA: Kendall Hunt.

Words of Wisdom

W hen I asked award-winning principals to share some of their general words of wisdom, I expected to hear many of the tried and true sayings such as "You can't expect what you don't inspect." Instead, they submitted a wide range of general words of wisdom that are guidelines for effective professional and personal settings.

In addition to guiding our work, quotations have many uses to encourage and communicate important ideas in a quick and often memorable way. Use them in your newsletters, staff memos, daily announcements, in your talks with students, faculty, parents, and at community functions. John Blaydes (2003), in his book *The Educator's Book of Quotes,* writes that "quotes are nuggets of wit and wisdom that motivate and inspire" (p. vii). Use these to do just that—to motivate and inspire, and add your own to the list.

WORDS OF WISDOM FROM PRINCIPALS TO PRINCIPALS

• One role a school leader needs to play is as a model of social justice. How else can we make a statement about how people should treat one another? It is a principal's responsibility to be proactive about social justice! (Elizabeth Neale)

- If you're not observing in classrooms, always have your door open and be ready to help teachers, parents, and students. (Sharon Roemer)

- One of my esteemed colleagues advises, "Live in the moment." (Rod Smith)

- Keep your priorities in line: God, family, school (students, staff, and parents). (Rod Smith)

- New principals should know that much of what principals do all day are things they don't teach you in principal school. In middle schools today, much of the time is spent on the 3 B's—buses, bathrooms, and bellies!! (Gene M. Solomon)

- Enjoy life. This is not a dress rehearsal. (Carol J. Lark)

- Students don't care how much you know until they know how much you care. (Lori Musser)

- If you lead an at-risk school, make it worth the drive for your teachers. (Carol J. Lark)

- Never forget what it was like in the classroom, and be the kind of principal you always wanted as a teacher. (Carol J. Lark)

- I like the wisdom of Harriet Beecher Stowe: "When you get into a tight place and everything goes against you till it seems you could not hold on a minute longer, never give up then, for that is just the time that the tide will turn." (Stephany Bourne)

- We all introduce new ideas each school year, but always try to do something new with faculty meetings: move the day, change the time or location. It makes for better listeners and keeps you from getting stale. (Kathleen Genovese Haworth)

- Keep in mind that leadership is a process. You must enjoy the process, or the stress from all the challenges makes it very frustrating. (Mary Kay Sommers)

- Learn to delegate and help teachers be leaders in your school. This creates a full learning and productive community. (Mary Kay Sommers)

- If there is a problem at school, I reflect on how a positive can result—and it usually does. Remember, turn your constraint into a positive. (Michele Pecina)

- It is a new day today. Remember the 3 P's as we touch the lives of children: Be positive, productive, and present. (Kim Boelkes)

- Always remember to maintain the balance between home and school. (Gloria L. Kumagai)

- All of us need to work smarter *and* harder! The work is not getting any easier. (Gloria L. Kumagai)

- The principal is the visible model of the school's heart and soul. (Dawn Smith)

- You can't just talk about it—you have to *be* about it! (Dawn Smith)

- Take the challenge—make it happen! (Dawn Smith)

- Use your own best judgment at all times. (John Ciesluk)

- The good is the enemy of the best. (Ursina Swanson)

- Leverage the good work your colleagues do. (Ursina Swanson)

- Common sense is not very common. (Ursina Swanson)

- I can't ask teachers to work harder, but I can ask them to work smarter. (Donald Greg Wood)

- The most important thing that we do is develop and utilize relationships in the community, among students, parents, faculty, and staff. (Donald Greg Wood)

- A principal's most important responsibilities are to hire quality staff and make sure they have what they need to do high-quality work. (Jane Hoskins Roberts)

- Have faith in yourself. You *can* do this! (Marla W. McGhee)

- For teachers: Be impeccable with your word. (Ramona S. Trevino)

- For teachers: Don't make assumptions. (Ramona S. Trevino)

- For students: Do your best. That is all we ever ask. (Ramona S. Trevino)

- What can I do to help? (Linda Webb)

- What do you think the real problem is? (Linda Webb)

- The principal is on your team. (Ann Porter)

- Administrators are definitely lifelong learners. When you feel confident with the material, spread the word to others—it's contagious! (Gina Segobiano)

- If you want a teacher's mind, you must first have his or her heart. (Scott Hollinger)

- Don't ask me to do what you will not do yourself. (Orquidia Hathaway)

- As principal, I am not a "leader" or a "boss." I am a facilitator of information, training, support, assistance, conflict management, intervention, counseling, coaching, and the list never ends. (Orquidia Hathaway)

- No whining. (Orquidia Hathaway)

WORDS OF WISDOM REFLECTION
1. What words of wisdom guide my professional practice?   2. What words of wisdom guide my personal practice?   3. What words of wisdom listed here would be most helpful for me?   4. What can I do to incorporate this (or these) truth(s) in my personal and professional life?

Reference

Blaydes, J. (2003). *The educator's book of quotes.* Thousand Oaks, CA: Corwin.

Recommended Reading List

The man who does not read good books has no advantage over the man who cannot read them.

—Mark Twain

When I asked principals to submit books that they felt every principal should read to be more effective, many of the books were the same. So instead of listing the book and who suggested it, I compiled all of their suggestions into this one list. Certainly this list does not include all the great books that have supported principals in their quest to be effective, but it is a great place to begin.

Avi. (1993). *Nothing but the truth: A documentary novel.* New York: HarperCollins.

Bennis, W. (1999). *Managing people is like herding cats.* Provo, UT: Executive Excellence.

Blanchard, K., & Johnson, S. (1981). *The one minute manager.* New York: William Morrow.

Blanchard, K., & Lorber, R. (1984). *Putting the one minute manager to work.* New York: William Morrow.

Blanchard, K., Zigarmi, P., & Zigmari, D. (1985). *Leadership and the one minute manager.* New York: William Morrow.

Booth, D., Fullan, M., & Rowsell, J. (2002). *The literacy principal: Leading, supporting, and assessing reading and writing initiatives.* Markham, ON: Pembroke.

Carter, S. C. (2000). *No excuses: Lessons from 21 high performing high poverty schools.* Washington, DC: Heritage Foundation.

Collins, J. (2001). *Good to great.* New York: HarperCollins.

Connors, N. (2001). *If you don't feed the teachers, they'll eat the students! Guide to success for administrators and teachers.* Hauppauge, NY: Barron's Educational Series.

Covey, S. (1995). *The 7 habits of highly effective people.* New York: St. Martin's Griffin.

DePorter, B., Reardon, M., & Singer-Nourie, S. (1999). *Quantum teaching: Orchestrating student success.* Boston: Allyn & Bacon.

DuFour, R. (1998). *Promoting learning communities at work: Best practices for enhancing student achievement.* Alexandria, VA: Association of Supervision and Curriculum Development.

Dunklee, D. (2000). *If you want to lead, not just manage: A primer for principals.* Thousand Oaks, CA: Corwin.

Fullan, M. (2003). *The moral imperative of school leadership.* Thousand Oaks, CA: Sage.

Gallagher, D. R., Bagin, D., & Kindred, L. W. (1997). *The school and community relations.* Boston: Allyn & Bacon.

Gore, A. (2000). *You can be happy: The essential guide to a healthy body, mind, and soul.* Thousand Oaks, CA: Corwin.

Gupton, S. (2003). *The instructional leadership toolbox: A handbook for improving practice.* Thousand Oaks, CA: Corwin.

Harris, S. (2004). *BRAVO Principal: Building relationships with actions that value others.* Larchmont, NY: Eye on Education.

Harwayne, S. (1999). *Going public.* Portsmouth, NH: Heinemann.

Holcolm, E. (2000). *Asking the right questions: Techniques for collaboration and school change.* Thousand Oaks, CA: Sage.

Kovalik, S., & Olsen, K. (2002). *Exceeding expectations: A user's guide to implementing brain research in the classroom.* Covington, WA: Books for Educators.

Kroeger, O., & Thuesen, J. (1989). *Type talk: The 16 personality types that determine how we live, love, and work.* New York: Dell.

Kroeger, O., Thuesen, J., & Rutledge, H. (2002). *Type talk at work: How the 16 personality types determine your success on the job.* New York: Dell.

Lundin, S., Christensen, J., & Paul, H. (2000). *FISH! A remarkable way to boost morale and improve results.* New York: Hyperion.

Lundin, S., Christensen, J., & Paul, H. (2002). *FISH! tales: Bite-sized stories: Unlimited possibilities.* New York: Hyperion.

Lundin, S., Christensen, J., & Paul, H. (2003). *FISH! sticks*. New York: Hyperion.

Marzano, R. (2003). *What works in schools: Translating research into action*. Alexandria, VA: Association of Supervision and Curriculum Development.

Marzano, R., Marzano, J., & Pickering, D. (2003). *Classroom management that works: Research-based strategies for every teacher*. Alexandria, VA: Association of Supervision and Curriculum Development.

Marzano, R., Pickering, D., & Pollock, J. (2001). *Classroom instruction that works: Research-based strategies for increasing student achievement*. Alexandria, VA: Association of Supervision and Curriculum Development.

Maxwell, J. (2001). *17 essential qualities of a team player: Becoming the kind of person every team wants*. Nashville, TN: Thomas Nelson.

Maxwell, J. (2004). *Today matters*. Boston: Warner Books.

McLain, S. (2002). *All business is show business*. Nashville, TN: Rutledge Hill Press.

Monroe, L. (1999). *Nothing's impossible: Leadership lessons from inside and outside the classroom*. New York: Public Affairs.

National Association of Elementary School Principals. (2001). *Leading learning communities: Standards for what principals should know and be able to do* (video series). Alexandria, VA: Author.

National Association of Elementary School Principals & Education Research Services. (2001). *Essentials for principals: Developing and maintaining high staff morale*. Alexandria, VA: Author.

Payne, R. (2001). *A framework for understanding poverty*. Highlands, TX: Aha! Process.

Phillips, D. T. (1993). *Lincoln on leadership: Executive strategies for tough times*. Boston: Warner Books.

Reeves, D. (2002). *The daily disciplines of leadership: How to improve student achievement, staff motivation, and personal organization*. San Francisco: Jossey-Bass.

Reeves, D. (2003). *Assessing educational leaders: Evaluating performance for improved individual and organizational results*. Thousand Oaks, CA: Sage.

Reeves, D. (2004). *Accountability for learning: How teachers and school leaders can take charge*. Alexandria, VA: Association of Supervision and Curriculum Development.

Rothman, R. (2001–2002). Closing the achievement gap: How schools are making it happen. *Journal of the Annenberg Challenge, 5*(2). Retrieved September 14, 2004, from www.annenbergchallenge.org/pubs/cj/gap_cj.htm

Ruiz, D. M. (1997). *The four agreements: A practical guide to personal freedom*. San Francisco: Amber-Allen.

Schmoker, M. (1999). *Results: The key to continuous school improvement.* Alexandria, VA: Association of Supervision and Curriculum Development.

Sollman, C., Emmons, B., & Paolini, J. (1994). *Through the cracks.* Worcester, MA: Davis.

Sommers, W., Ghere, G., & Montie, J. (2001). *Reflective practice to improve schools: An action guide for educators.* Thousand Oaks, CA: Sage.

Whitaker, T. (2003). *What great principals do differently: Fifteen things that matter most.* Larchmont, NY: Eye on Education.

Whitaker, T., Whitaker, B., & Lumpa, D. (2000). *Motivating and inspiring teachers.* Larchmont, NY: Eye on Education.

Williams, B. (Ed.). (2004). *Closing the achievement gap: A vision for changing beliefs and practices.* Alexandria, VA: Association of Supervision and Curriculum Development.

Wong, H., & Breaux, A. L. (2003). *New teacher induction: How to train, support, and retain new teachers.* Mountain View, CA: Harry K. Wong.

Zemelman, S. H., Daniels, H., & Hyde, A. (1998). *Best practice: New standards for teaching and learning in America's schools.* Portsmouth, NH: Heinemann.

RECOMMENDED READING LIST REFLECTION

1. Of the recommended books, which ones have I already read?
2. Of the recommended books, which ones do I want to read?
3. What books have I read that I think are a must for effective principals to read?

10

Conclusion

Man's mind, stretched to a new idea, never goes back to its original dimensions.

—Oliver Wendell Holmes

W hen I began this project, I looked forward eagerly to the many ideas that these award-winning principals would share. While I suggested best practice categories, such as parent programs, diversity, instruction, and others, I also asked principals to feel free to create their own categories. Most of their ideas fell into the six categories of leadership, shaping campus culture, collaborating and communicating, effective instructional programs, school improvement plans, and at-risk programs, which became the chapter titles. There were a few general suggestions that I included in Chapter 7. The fact that elementary school principals' best practice ideas followed this pattern suggests the following for elementary school principals of today who want to lead effective schools:

- Principals must understand that effective leadership is vital to the success of the school.
- Principals must know how to shape a positive campus culture.

- Principals must know how to collaborate and communicate effectively with the school community.
- Principals must be able to oversee the implementation of an effective instructional program.
- Principals must be alert to improving the school.
- Principals are responsible for *all* students to have optimum learning opportunities at school.

Certainly these are not the only important strategies and components for an effective school, but according to these principals, these six areas are clearly foundational to a principal's success and, ultimately, to a school's success.

However, as I considered the principals' responses in this project, I was struck by three themes that resonated in every response at some point. These themes were (1) we, not me; (2) people, not programs; and (3) students, not schools.

WE, NOT ME

Rarely, if ever, did principals share their best practice ideas by talking about what "I" did for "my" school. Instead, according to Marla W. McGhee, we "rolled up our shirt sleeves and worked side by side." In this way, principals shared what "we" did at "our" school. For example, Kim Boelkes says that "inservice became part of our everyday life," "our challenge became . . . ," and "we embraced. . . ." Lori Musser comments that "we work together . . . ," "our teachers attend . . . ," and "we realize. . . ." Cindy Gipson even includes the students in this inclusive language when she points out that to get ready for state tests, "we practice minisample tests." Stephany Bourne describes "forming a team" to address bullying and other poor student behaviors.

Michele Pecina encourages teachers to identify and enlarge their repertoire of professional knowledge. Carol J. Lark worked with a university professor and a team of teachers to make the school safer. Mary Kay Sommers, in one brief paragraph, mentions "we" five times as she describes what is happening at school. Ursina Swanson does not allow interruptions, because teachers' time with students is valuable. Karen Lyon leads a wellness staff development because she recognizes the importance of a healthy faculty.

Donald Greg Wood synthesizes the idea of "we, not me" most pointedly. In our telephone interview, he stressed the importance of sharing information with the faculty and listening to their ideas, because "their decisions are effective." In other words, effective principals involve many stakeholders in decisions that create successful schools. Successful principals cannot lead schools alone. The team consists of faculty, students, parents, and community stakeholders. Best practices that are implemented at a school are part of a team effort. Ann Porter even wore an apron when she helped in the lunchroom to emphasize the message that the principal is part of the team. It's we, not me.

People, Not Programs

When the principals shared their ideas for creating an effective school, they wrote or talked about what the people at their school were doing, rather than what the programs were doing for their school. Rod Smith's faculty implemented a program called Authors & Illustrators, whose purpose was to "teach *students* the value of writing." Dawn Smith added a communication tool so that parents will be informed "of what is coming up academically and what their children will miss." Robert W. Fowls matches up younger students with older student "buddies" for reading but primarily to "develop relationships." Paul Young reminds us that art programs "provide students reasons to come to school." Cynthia Eliser's advice focuses on life outside of school, and Gloria L. Kumagai suggests the need for balance between home and school. Jane Hoskins Roberts emphasizes the importance of involving staff and parent groups in the complete school improvement plan.

Each time Gene M. Solomon describes programs at school, he points out that they are for students and family. Orquidia

Hathaway led her faculty to adopt a vision that focuses on building children's strengths. Sharon Roemer involves parents through a reading program. Carol Loflin schedules an Author's Lunch to encourage student writing, but, more important, to "get to know students as writers." Sharon Roemer has implemented a self-esteem program to "give children the tools for developing skills." Rick Ivers uses the Literacy Lab for "students to find reading success."

Award-winning elementary school principals understand that people are the most important resource at the school. Gina Segobiano points out that the development of sincere, supportive relationships "establishes an educational climate that is one of mutual respect and appreciation." Sharon Vestermark cautions us that input from stakeholders must be valued and we should not just rubber-stamp staff wishes. Programs are important, but the people who implement a program hold the key to its success or failure. Schools are about people, not programs.

STUDENTS, NOT SCHOOLS

As elementary school principals shared best practice ideas at their schools, they emphasized what they were doing for their students, not what they were doing for their school, a mission that a teacher at the school led by Ramona S. Trevino called "majestic." Kathleen Genovese Haworth points out that faculty "take a personal interest in the students," Exerta T. Mackie's faculty address "the needs of the whole child," and John Ciesluk "greets all students by name every day." Keith Owen describes an intensive reading model for the purpose of providing "intensive remediation to those students who needed it."

Elizabeth Neale shared with me in a telephone interview that she asked her district to send all of the ELL children who did not speak English to her campus because her faculty would "integrate the children into the classroom immediately." Dan Coram emphasizes that assessment is used to "ensure mastery of basic skills *child by child*."

Award-winning elementary school principals understand that education should be about students, not schools. Linda Webb points out that the "success of students is reliant upon the relationships within the school." If a child is not successful at school, it doesn't matter if the school is an award-winning school, a Distinguished school, an Exemplary school, or any other quality designation; for that child, the school is a failure. Education is about students, not schools.

The best practice ideas from these award-winning elementary school principals provide a variety of ways to make principals more effective. We encourage you to consider these ideas and reflect on how you might use them in your school. Brainstorm ways that you might personalize these suggestions for your school. Consider ways that you might improve on these ideas and motivate and inspire everyone on your campus to reach an even higher standard of teaching and learning. After all, as award-winning principal Scott Hollinger wrote, principals have the marvelous challenge of "guiding more by inspiration than by directive."

Danish author and scientist Piet Hein reminds us that "the road to wisdom . . . is plain and simple to express: Err and err and err again but less and less and less." The ideas in this book will help principals err less and less; they might even help you become an award-winning principal. But for sure, they will help you lead your school to reach new successes for students.

REFERENCE

Hein, P. The road to wisdom. Retrieved February 1, 2005 from http://www.ctaz.com/~dmn1/hein.htm

Index

**CORWIN
PRESS**

The Corwin Press logo—a raven striding across an open book—represents the union of courage and learning. Corwin Press is committed to improving education for all learners by publishing books and other professional development resources for those serving the field of K–12 education. By providing practical, hands-on materials, Corwin Press continues to carry out the promise of its motto: **"Helping Educators Do Their Work Better."**